THE BATTLE FOR IWO JIMA

ROBERT LECKIE was born in Philadelphia, the youngest in an Irish-Catholic family of eight children. Growing up in Rutherford, New Jersey, Robert Leckie got his first writing job covering football for the Bergen *Evening Record* in Hackensack. Upon hearing of the Japanese bombing of Pearl Harbor, Leckie joined the Marines and served nearly three years in the Pacific theater, winning eight battle stars, four Presidential Unit Citations, the Purple Heart, and the Naval Commendation Medal with Combat V. His wartime experiences formed the basis of his acclaimed first book, *Helmet For My Pillow*.

Following World War II, Leckie continued his journalistic career, writing for the Associated Press and the New York *Daily News* and serving as an editor for MGM newsreels. Leckie is also the author of *March to Glory, The General* and numerous other military history and historical fiction books. Robert Leckie died on December 24, 2001.

AVAILABLE NOW

THE BATTLE FOR IWO JIMA

By
ROBERT LECKIE

Maps by Ted Burwell

ibooks

new york
www.ibooks.net

DISTRIBUTED BY SIMON & SCHUSTER

An ibooks, inc. Book

Distributed by Simon & Schuster, Inc.
1230 Avenue of the Americas, New York, NY 10020

ibooks, inc.
24 West 25th Street
New York, NY 10010

The ibooks World Wide Web Site address is:
http://www.ibooks.net

Front Cover Design by Matt Postawa

ISBN: 0-7434-8682-X
First ibooks printing August 2004
10 9 8 7 6 5 4 3 2

To Angelo Bertelli and Douglas Boyd
Two Good Marines Who Fought at Iwo Jima

CONTENTS

1. THE MARINES GO IN   1

2. THE IMPORTANCE OF IWO   7

3. THE TERRIBLE FIRST DAY   21

4. THE FLAG FLIES AT SURIBACHI   39

5. THE UP-ISLAND DRIVE   55

6. INTO THE MEATGRINDER   75

7. BREAKTHROUGH   91

8. 'TILL THE LAST MAN   107

ORDER OF EVENTS IN THE INVASION   123

NOTE ON UNIT STRENGTH   127

MARINES WHO WON THE MEDAL OF HONOR 129

THE BATTLE FOR IWO JIMA

CHAPTER 1

THE MARINES GO IN

THE BATTLE FOR IWO JIMA

On February 19, 1945, the United States brought the war in the Pacific to the front doorstep of Japan. Iwo Jima was a tiny dark island four and a half miles long and two and a half miles wide. Located only 660 miles south of Tokyo, it looked from the air like a lopsided, black pork chop.

On the bright, clear morning of that fateful Monday, a vast armada of 485 American ships completely surrounded Iwo Jima. Battleships and cruisers stood off in the distance to batter Japanese positions and pin down the enemy so that the assault troops might get safely ashore. Great flashes of orange flame erupted from the ships' guns as they sent huge shells howling toward their targets. Closer still, graceful destroyers seemed to dance off shore, dueling Japanese gun batteries, while rocket ships turned broadside to unleash flights of missiles.

Out of sight were the aircraft carriers, from whose decks had come the bombers and fighters that were also striking at Iwo. The planes flashed in and out of clouds of smoke and dust with bombs, rockets and machine guns. In addition, a formation of Liberators had flown in from faraway bases in the Marianas to make the little island quiver and shake with "carpets" of big bombs.

It did not seem possible that anything—especially

human beings—could survive on little Iwo. And indeed there was no answering fire from the tiny dark island. All was strangely quiet. To the south, the volcano Mount Suribachi rose 550 feet above the sea. Just north of it, on the island's east coast, were the landing beaches: silent, black and sinister. Then fading away to the north was a jumble of ridges rising to a high plateau. This was Iwo Jima, or Sulphur Island, which 70,000 United States Marines had come to claim for the Stars and Stripes.

As the aerial bombardment slackened, the first waves of Marines prepared to attack. Holding their rifles and machine guns, their flame throwers and bazookas, they filed down to the bottom deck of their landing ships. There they clambered aboard amphibious tractors, or "amtracks." The amtracks, which the Japanese called "little boats with wheels" because of the gears on which their tracks turned, could churn through water and roll over land. Like great jaws, the forward bow doors of the landing ships yawned and opened wide. There was a great coughing and a roar of motors starting. Inside the landing ships the air became blue with smoke. Some of the Marines had begun to sweat, even though the air was crisp and cool. As they brushed aside beads of perspiration, they smeared the antiflash cream they had put on their faces to prevent burns.

Then the amtracks waddled forward. Like so many ducks, they spilled out of their mother ships, dropped into the water and formed landing circles. Around and around they circled, waiting for the order to attack. The order came. One by one the amtracks swung wide into the attack line. Gradually gathering speed, they went churning toward Iwo's terraced beaches. The sea bombardment was lifting; the last aerial strike had come and gone. The sound of the amtrack motors was rising to a roar. Marines crouched anxiously below the gunwales, braced for the enemy's long-awaited answering fire. None came.

Beneath them, the Marines felt a jolt and a lurch. Then they were on their feet—weapons held high—vaulting over the side and sinking ankle-deep into the warm, black sands of Iwo Jima.

CHAPTER 2

THE IMPORTANCE OF IWO

THE BATTLE FOR IWO JIMA

In the fall of 1944, the American high command had decided to capture Iwo Jima. The little island was important because it was only 660 miles from Tokyo. Iwo and the bigger island of Okinawa were to be used as bases for the final invasion of Japan.

But after the big B-29 Superfort bombers began to raid Japan from the recently captured chain of islands called the Marianas, the Americans realized that it was imperative to capture Iwo Jima as soon as possible. For Iwo lay on a direct line between the Marianas and Japan, and the Japanese on the island could give advance warning of the bombers' approach. The enemy would then put up massive antiaircraft barrages and "stack" fighter planes high in the sky, waiting to pounce on the B-29s. If the fighters could not shoot down a B-29, then they tried to ram it. As a result, the Americans were losing far too many Superforts over Japan. Others were so crippled by the attacks that they crashed into the sea during the long 1500-mile trip back to the Marianas.

The American commanders saw at once that if they captured Iwo their bombers could fly closer to Japan without being detected. Next, Iwo would give them a base for fighter planes, which could then escort the bombers to and from Japan. Finally, and most important, Iwo Jima would be an ideal halfway-haven for crippled B-29s trying to limp back to base. By landing on Iwo's emergency fields, they could be saved, along with their priceless crews. If they crashed between Japan and Iwo, or between Iwo and the Marianas, then at least the crews might be saved. Moreover, if Iwo became a regular stop-off on return flights, the bombers could carry less gasoline and more bombs.

These were the advantages of capturing Iwo Jima. Not only were they great, but they could be realized almost immediately. This does not happen often in war. Usually, an objective has long-range benefits.

The invasion of this little dot of land would also strike a blow at the enemy second only to the invasion of Japan itself. For Iwo Jima was Japanese soil. No foreigner had been known to set foot on it. All the other islands held by the Japanese had once belonged to some other country. For example, Tarawa had been a British colony and the Philippines had been an American territory. But Iwo Jima was part of the Prefecture of Tokyo, one of Japan's 47 provinces. That was why the emperor had sent his best soldiers and one of his best generals out to defend it.

THE BATTLE FOR IWO JIMA

Lieutenant General Tadamichi Kuribayashi was a moon-faced, pudgy man who was fond of animals and children. He was also a stern soldier. His round belly, as one Japanese newspaper observed, was "packed full of very strong fighting spirit." Kuribayashi had served in the cavalry, the elite of the Japanese army. He had fought with distinction in China before returning home to Tokyo. There, in May of 1944, he was summoned into the august presence of Premier Hideki Tojo and informed that he was to command at Iwo Jima. "Only you among all the generals are qualified and capable of holding this post," Tojo said. "The entire army and the nation will depend on you for the defense of that key position."

General Kuribayashi replied that he was honored to be chosen. Then, in the formal Japanese way, he bowed solemnly and left to say good-by to his wife and children. He did not tell them what he believed in his heart: that he would not return from Iwo Jima. But he did write to his brother: "I may not return alive from this assignment, but let me assure you that I shall fight to the best of my ability, so that no disgrace will be brought upon our family."

General Kuribayashi's conviction of a fight to the death became stronger after the Marianas fell. These island outposts were often called the Pearl Harbor of Japan. Their loss during July and August of 1944 so shocked the nation that Premier Tojo had to resign. Tojo had always told the emperor and the people that the Americans were soft and would not have the courage to fight a long and costly war. They would quickly give up, he said, and agree to a peace that would leave Japan in possession of most of her stolen empire. But the course of the war had taken a different turn. Now, two and a half years after the Japanese sneak attack on Pearl Harbor, the "soft" Yankees stood triumphant in the Marianas—only 1,500 miles from Japan! As Tojo knew, they would soon be using their B-29 bombers to raid the homeland itself, and because he failed to prevent this threat he had to step down.

Meanwhile, the Marianas disaster made it plain to General Kuribayashi that he could not prevent the enemy from landing on Iwo. Obviously, the Americans had too many ships, planes, guns and men for that. But Kuribayashi was one of Japan's most intelligent strategists. He devised a new battle plan which departed from the usual Japanese methods of dealing with invasion from the sea.

Throughout the war, the Japanese strategy for defending an island had been to "destroy the enemy at the water's edge." That meant trying to prevent them from landing. If, however, the enemy did make a successful landing, then the Japanese hit them hard during the night with a wild bayonet charge. Because the Japanese soldiers screamed, *Banzai!"* as they charged forward, these night attacks became known as *banzai* charges. They never succeeded, however. In fact, the Japanese would lose so many men in one of these *banzai* charges, that they wouldn't have enough troops left to defend their island.

General Kuribayashi intended to do just the opposite. He would let the Americans land unopposed. He would give them about an hour to become packed and crowded on the flat, black sands between Mount Suribachi in the south and his own headquarters on the high ground in the north. Then he would open up with every weapon he had and turn Iwo's middle ground into a fearful slaughter pen. To do this, he began to transform Iwo Jima into what was to become one of the strongest fixed positions in the history of warfare.

In the south, under Suribachi, the Japanese began to build a seven-story gallery. Caves five feet wide, 35 feet long and five feet high were dug into the sides of the mountain. All the entrances were angled to guard against enemy fire, and the caves were cleverly vented at the top to draw off steam or sulphur fumes. Sometimes, as the Japanese soldiers worked to build their honeycomb of concrete and steel, the heat from the volcano forced the temperature up to 160 degrees. Into these positions the general put much artillery and about 2,000 men.

In the middle ground off the landing beaches he put perhaps another 1,500 soldiers. Here, they built numerous machine-gun positions with thick walls and roofs of reinforced concrete. These fortifications were made to look like innocent hummocks of sand.

The remainder of Kuribayashi's 21,000 men and guns went into the high ground in the north. Two heavy lines of forts, pillboxes and tunnels were built across the island. Giant blockhouses were constructed. Natural caverns, big enough to hold whole companies, were reinforced and electrified. Even little cracks in the rock were widened to hold single snipers. Tunnels ran everywhere, connecting the various positions, and all this construction was cleverly concealed so that the attacking Americans would not know that they were inside a network of guns until they were under fire.

In addition, General Kuribayashi made it plainly known to his soldiers that he expected them to fight to the death. He issued the "Iwo Jima Courageous Battle Vow," which the men recited regularly:

> Above all else we shall dedicate ourselves and our entire strength to the defense of this island.
> We shall grasp bombs, charge the enemy tanks and destroy them.
> We shall infiltrate into the midst of the enemy and annihilate them.
> With every salvo we will, without fail, kill the enemy.
> Each man will make it his duty to kill 10 of the enemy before dying.
> Until we are destroyed to the last man, we shall harass the enemy by guerrilla tactics.

General Kuribayashi also was very strict about cover and concealment. Every position had to be underground or fortified. He gave orders that, when the American warships and airplanes began their preinvasion bombardment, the Japanese guns were not to fire back and thus give away their positions. Because of the general's precautions, the Navy and the Air Corps mistakenly believed that they had knocked out many enemy targets.

The Marines who were to take Iwo Jima had no illusions, however. Most of the officers and men of the Fifth Amphibious Corps, made up of the 3rd, 4th, and 5th Marine divisions, were veterans of the Pacific War. They had been at Bougainville or the Marshalls or the Marianas, as well as many other islands, and they knew that a concrete pillbox is destroyed only by a direct hit. This is difficult for naval guns to achieve, for they fire on a flat line, and airplanes are usually too high to drop their bombs directly on top of a pillbox roof.

No, the Marines knew that in the end they would have to do the job. They would have to go in on foot with rifle and grenade. They knew, too, that all 70,000 of them would be needed to defeat 21,000 well-protected, well-hidden, well-armed Japanese. In assault from the sea, the invading force usually needs a five-to-one superiority. Yet, on a little island like Iwo, it can be dangerous to have too many men in one place. Too great a concentration of troops may offer the enemy too many targets. That was why General Kuribayashi had perhaps just the right number.

So the Marines knew that they had drawn the toughest mission in their long and glorious career. And no one knew this better than Lieutenant General Holland M. Smith, their commander. General Smith looked like a college professor, with his gold-rimmed eyeglasses, big nose and gray mustache. But he had a hot temper, which had earned him the nickname of "Howlin' Mad" Smith. Even so, General Smith was very fond of his Marines. There were tears in his eyes when he announced that there would probably be 15,000 dead and wounded at Iwo. "We have never failed," he said, "and I don't believe we shall fail here."

Major General Harry Schmidt was to command the Marines once they were ashore. A stocky, silent man who often scowled, he told the reporters: "We expect to get on their tails and keep on their tails until we chop them off." General Schmidt's plan was to attack two divisions abreast, with a third in reserve. The 5th would go in on the left, the 4th on the right.

Major General Clifton B. Cates led the 4th. One of the oldest "salts" in the Marine Corps, he had fought at Belleau Wood in World War One and had commanded a regiment on Guadalcanal. He was a soft-spoken man who was tense before a battle, but once the fighting began, he relaxed. Cates's 4th Division had been given the dangerous assignment of landing beneath the guns of the northeastern cliffs, and the general was so struck by the enormity of the task that he said: "You know, if I knew the name of the man on the extreme right of the right-hand squad of the right-hand company of the right-hand battalion, I 'd recommend him for a medal before we go in."

The 5th Division, which was to attack on the left and capture Suribachi, had never been in battle before as a unit. But many of its Marines had combat experience. One of these veterans was "Manila John" Basilone, the gallant sergeant who had won the Medal of Honor on Guadalcanal. Major General Keller Rockey commanded the 5th. He, too, was a veteran—but of Belleau Wood. Now, big Keller Rockey was eager to earn another set of spurs in this war.

The 3rd Marine Division was to be in "floating reserve." That is, its units would stay aboard ship off Iwo until they were needed to turn the tide of battle or to relieve some tired units. Major General Graves B. Erskine led the 3rd. He was a strong, handsome man, and his Marines had nicknamed him "The Big E" after the famous aircraft carrier *Enterprise*.

Commanding all of these men, as well as all of the ships and sailors of the fleet, was Vice Admiral Richmond Kelly Turner. One of the saltiest American sailors afloat, Admiral Turner had also led the amphibious force that invaded Guadalcanal in August, 1942, to begin the American counterattack across the Pacific. His job was to get the invasion force safely to Iwo Jima and to keep it supplied and protected after it was put ashore. Sharp-tongued, beetle-browed, given to prowling the bridge of his flagship in an old bathrobe, Kelly Turner was the kind of perfectionist who would not hesitate to tell a coxswain how to handle his boat. He had asked for "only three good days" at Iwo, and he was delighted that the first day was one of these. That fateful morning the welcome news was broadcast to the fleet from his flagship, *Eldorado:* "Very light swells. Boating: excellent. Visibility: excellent."

So the Marines went roaring in to Iwo, and for the space of a half hour or more it appeared that their report would be "Landing: excellent."

Marine landing craft approach Iwo Jima.
Mt. Suribachi is on the far left.
Courtesy USMC

Aerial photograph of a pre-invasion bombing raid.
Courtesy USAF

Amtracks churn through the water,
waiting for the order to attack.
Courtesy USMC

General Kuribayashi on Iwo Jima.
Courtesy Mrs. Kuribayashi

A sketch of Hill 362A prepared by the Seabees.
The hill is seen from the north. Dotted lines indicate
underground tunnels and galleries.
Courtesy US Navy

The Japanese buried these "kettle" mines
on the beach in deadly abundance.
Courtesy USMC

Left to right: Lieutenant General Smith, Vice Admiral Turner and Rear Admiral Hill discuss invasions plans on Turner's flagship, *Eldorado*.
Courtesy USMC

This Marine was one of many killed
by intense sniper fire.
Courtesy USMC

The wounded are given first aid on
Iwo's tightly packed beaches.
Courtesy USMC

A marine uses his flame thrower to destroy one of the
sand-covered bunkers guarding Airfield Number One.
Courtesy USMC

This 37-millimeter gun has been set up at the edge of
Airfield Number One. The carrier plane in the background
has just dropped a bomb at the base of Mt. Suribachi.
Courtesy USMC

A supply-boat coxswain maneuvers his craft
up to the wreckage-strewn beach.
Courtesy USMC

Horrible Hank, with water pouring from the muzzle
of its 75-millimeter gun, lies just offshore
after an unsuccessful landing attempt.
Courtesy USMC

Marine engineers probe for mines.
White tapes mark the path for the tanks to follow.
Courtesy USMC

Men of the 7th Regiment, 2nd Battalion, 5th Division land on the beach during the afternoon of D day.
Courtesy USMC

Amtracks, bulldozers and ducks negotiate a
mine-free road while shore parties pass supplies
along a human conveyor belt.
Courtesy USMC

CHAPTER 3

THE TERRIBLE FIRST DAY

The only apparent difficulty on Iwo seemed to be the terraces of volcanic ash which wind and wave had heaped inland at heights up to 15 feet. Many of the armored amtracks, or "amtanks," could not climb them. Instead, they backed into the sea again, churned out, and turned to open fire on the island.

Troop amtracks, sending up showers of sand, tried to grind through the terraces. They too became stalled, and their marine passengers leaped out to continue inland afoot. Still there was no fire from the enemy. In came the second wave unopposed. The third... the fourth... Marines trudging inland through the warm, loose sand began to hope that the Japanese had fled the island. But as the American invaders climbed the terraces and began to swarm across the broad flatland beyond, the Japanese gunners opened fire.

At first it came as a ragged rattle of machine-gun bullets, growing gradually louder and fiercer until at last all the pent-up fury of a hundred hurricanes seemed to be breaking upon the heads of the Americans. Shells screeched and crashed, every hummock spat automatic fire and the very soil underfoot erupted with hundreds of exploding land mines. In everyone's ears was the song of unseen steel: the shriek of shells, the sigh of bullets, the sobbing of the big projectiles and the whizzing of shrapnel. Marines walking erect crumpled and fell. Concussion lifted them and slammed them down, or tore them apart—sometimes hurling a man's arms or legs thirty or forty feet away from his body.

There were few places to hide—only the shallow depressions in the sand caused by bomb and shell explosions. There was almost no place to dig. Iwo's peculiar sands, like fine buckshot, slid back into the foxholes and filled them in again. Nor was it wise to take shelter behind a sand hummock. A Marine captain sat on one and called out an order to advance. The blasting of a five-inch gun beneath him knocked him unconscious.

Nevertheless, the American Marines pressed forward. Tadamichi Kuribayashi had given them time to come ashore, and that was all they needed. By the time his gunners opened up, the Marines were 200 to 300 yards inland.

On the left flank, under the fire from Suribachi, the 5th Division had begun to push across the narrowest part of the island. Manila John Basilone called to his machine-gun section: "C'mon, you guys! Let's get these guns off the beach." They obeyed, and ran into the blast of an exploding mortar shell that killed Basilone and four others.

Here, too, big Captain Dwayne "Bobo" Mears attacked an enemy pillbox blocking his company's advance. He knocked it out, using only his pistol. But an enemy bullet opened a gash in his neck. Mears waited for it to be bandaged, and returned to the attack. Now a bullet ripped through his jaw. Blood spurted out and clotted the sand. Mears kept on. But at last he sank to the sand. A private ran up and tried to protect him. "Get out of here," Mears gasped. "I'll be all right." Then Navy medical corpsmen picked him up, and for a while it looked as if he might be saved, but the gallant captain later died aboard ship.

Everywhere now rose the cry, "Corpsman! Corpsman!" as Marines fell stricken. Rushing forward with sulpha and bandages, heedless of the enemy fire, the corpsmen bound up the wounds of the fallen and ticketed them for evacuation to the hospital ships out in the water. Sometimes the corpsmen arrived too late. Often, all too often, the young Marines quietly bled to death where they fell.

Still, the assault on the left was pressed forward, even though some of the 5th's battalions were down to one out of four original company commanders, and some platoons were being led by enlisted men. If a captain fell, a lieutenant took his place. If a platoon lost its lieutenant and NCOs, some young, and untried private would leap into the breach. Many Marines proved to be unexpectedly resourceful leaders that day.

Corporal Tony Stein, of the 28th Regiment, was one of these. Unusually handsome, he was also unusually tough. In fact, his nickname was "Tough Tony." Corporal Stein had been a toolmaker in civilian life, and back in Hawaii he had fashioned a special weapon for himself from the wing gun of a wrecked Navy fighter. He called it a "stinger." Using his stinger, Tony Stein struck at pillbox after pillbox on the left flank. One after another he killed the defenders, leaving the position to be destroyed by Sergeant Merritt Savage, a demolitions expert, and Corporal Frederick Tabert, both of whom followed in Stein's rear.

Sometimes Tough Tony was so exciting in his one-man war across the island that his comrades stopped to watch him in admiration. But there was no stopping for Tony Stein. Running out of ammunition, he threw off his helmet, shucked his shoes and sprinted to the rear to get more bullets. He did this eight times, each time pausing to help a wounded Marine to an aid station. Finally, when the Japanese forced his platoon to pull back, Tony

Stein covered the withdrawal. Twice, his stinger was shot from his hands. But each time he retrieved it and fired on.

Behind Tony Stein's battalion came another battalion of the 28th Regiment. These Marines were horrified to find the beaches a litter of wrecked and burning vehicles. They passed the lifeless bodies of men who had landed before them, and tripped over severed limbs lying lonely and bloody in the sand. As the din of battle engulfed these men, they realized that their objective would be taken only at a terrible price.

One Marine platoon moved forward under Lieutenant John Wells. Soon they ran into a Japanese bunker. It looked like a harmless mound of sand. But it spat fire, and a Marine buckled and died. Moving to their right, Wells's platoon got out of the bunker's field of fire. The enemy guns could not swing far enough to their left to hit them. From this point, a Marine rushed in on the bunker's blind side with a "shaped" charge. This is an explosive shaped to concentrate most of its blast in a small area. It is provided with supports to keep the charge a certain distance from the target to be penetrated, and it looks something like a kettle on stilts. The Marine scrambled to the top of the mound and scooped out a hole in the sand. Planting the charge, he raced away for safety.

There was a roar, and the blast tore a hole in the bunker's roof. This was not enough to knock it out, however, and another Marine now dashed forward with a thermite, or heat, grenade. He dropped it down the hole. Instantly the grenade began to generate intense heat and smoke. The Japanese inside the bunker could not bear it. They threw open the door and came charging out through a billowing cloud of white smoke. As the enemy rushed out, the Marines cut them down.

Thus, either with such systematic tactics, or through the sheer bravery and dash of Marines like Tony Stein, the men of the 5th Division punched clear across the island. When they reached the western beaches, they had cut off Mount Suribachi to their left, or south.

On the right flank of the American assault line, the fighting was even fiercer. Here the Japanese gunners had the beaches "zeroed in." Marines landing there were as naked to their enemies as flies walking on a windowpane. Fire fell on them from their front and both flanks. It came from a rock quarry on the far right, from Suribachi on the far left and from pillboxes, blockhouses and spider traps straight ahead. In front of one battalion alone were two huge blockhouses and 50 pillboxes. This battalion was supposed to take Airfield Number One in the middle of the Iwo flatland. Its commander decided to wait until artillery arrived. But Sergeant Darrell Cole refused to wait.

He led his machine-gun section toward the field and into a network of enemy guns. Cole's Marines fired into the gun slits as they passed. Cole knocked out two pillboxes himself with hand grenades. Then three bunkers pinned his men down in a cross fire. Cole silenced the nearest one with a counter cross fire. The enemy threw grenades. So did Cole. Three times he struck at the remaining pillboxes, finally knocking them out. But then a bursting grenade killed Sergeant Darrell Cole.

Not all of the Marine companies penetrated the enemy line so rapidly. One company was pinned down in a hail of fire for 45 minutes while its agonized men watched their captain, John Kalen, slowly bleed to death in a hole ringed around by exploding steel. Behind this unit, the guns of the cruiser *Chester* tried to blast a path inland for the Marines. The *Chester*'s fire was directed by Lieutenant Commander Robert Kalen, who of course did not know that his brother was bleeding to death ashore. Before the day was over, command of this company changed hands four times.

As the enemy fire rose in fury so did the surf off all the beaches. Landing boats were caught up and hurled hard against the shore. They were wrecked, sunk or driven up on the beach, where they filled with water. Minute by minute the surf line was being turned into an impassable tangle of smashed boats, stalled and wrecked vehicles, bodies, crates, cartons and cans. From flank to flank the beachhead was marked by this long dark pile of debris, which surged with every wave. Offshore there was a swarm of landing boats. Every coxswain was convinced that he carried "hot" cargo; that is, badly needed supplies. All of them sought an opening in the tangle so that they could get ashore, unload and speed away from that place of exploding steel. In another hour or so, it might be impossible to get reinforcements or supplies ashore.

In the meantime, both Marine divisions had begun to call desperately for tanks. The big 15-ton Shermans could help turn the tide of battle. Their armor was thick enough to deflect most enemy missiles, and their 75-millimeter rifles were powerful enough to knock out most enemy positions. An hour after the invasion, 16 Shermans were landed in the 4th

Division's right-flank sector. But they had trouble getting through the beach terraces. On the 5th's left-flank beaches there was even more trouble. Lieutenant Henry Morgan's tank, named *Horrible Hank*, was lost when a big wave swamped the lighter which carried it. Lieutenant Morgan radioed his commander: "Horrible Hank sank." Then he went on to have two more tanks blown out from under him.

Everywhere the Shermans were being hit by shells. Few of them were knocked out, however; most of them continued to grind their way over the terraces. If they succeeded in getting over that obstacle, however, they entered deadly mine fields. Engineer troops had to precede the tanks on their knees, using their bayonets to poke for mines. They sought the mines by hand because mine detectors were not effective in the magnetic sand. Besides, most of the mines were made of a ceramic material instead of metal. So the gallant engineers gingerly cleared paths through the mines and marked them with white tape for the tanks.

Sometimes, if the tanks could not get through the terraces, the bulldozers cut paths for them. But the bulldozers were also shelled, and easily knocked out. Nevertheless, most of the Shermans got through. The Marine riflemen, however, greeted their arrival with mixed emotions. They knew what the tanks could do, but they also knew that the armored monsters would draw enemy fire. "It's a tossup whether to run away from them," said a corporal, "or crawl under them."

Even before the tanks came in, the Navy beachmaster parties came ashore. It was their job to organize the beaches so that the flow of supplies to the fighting front would be smooth and steady. One of these beachmaster parties came right in after the first wave of Marines. The men landed with colored flags, bull horns, radios, portable generators and sandbags. The generators were dug in and sandbagged. The bull horns were set up on tripods to bellow orders that could be heard by supply-boat coxswains above the roar of guns and the surf. The flags were used to mark off the different beaches assigned to various Marine regiments, and the radios relayed the requests of the Marines to the ships offshore.

The assault troops battling grimly into Iwo's defenses needed a wide variety of supplies. They required all kinds of ammunition, as well as fuel for their flame throwers, dynamite, barbed wire, water, grenades, gasoline and medical supplies. They also needed food rations. But there was never a question of which should come first—the "beans" or the "bullets." The bullets always went in ahead. To get these supplies into the hands of the Marines, roads from the beaches had to be cut through the sand terraces which had already blocked the passage of so many vehicles. To do this, a battalion of Seabees came into Iwo Jima.

Seabees are sailor-specialists from Naval Construction Battalions. Their colorful nickname comes from the abbreviation C.B. Many of these highly trained technicians and mechanics were men in their thirties—or forties—who had put their civilian skills and crafts at their country's service. Between the older Seabees and the youthful Marines there was a great bond of affection. They were the "old men" or the "kids" to each other.

Usually, Seabees had not come into an island until a day or two after the assault. But at Iwo Jima they arrived during the afternoon of D day! They were desperately needed to cut those roads through the terraces. Then supplies could be carried directly from the ships to the battlefield by amphibian trucks called DUKWS, or just plain "ducks." When the ducks emerged dripping from the water, they displayed rubber wheels like any other truck and were able to roll anywhere. At Iwo, they were driven by Negro soldiers, who were the only Army troops to participate in the battle.

So the Seabees in their bulldozers cut swaths through the terraces, and some of them were killed or wounded as they worked. One bulldozer driven by Alphenix Benard came into the right-flank beaches in a tank lighter. When the ramp banged down, Benard saw a pile of American bodies blocking his path. He hesitated, horrified. But behind him were another bulldozer, two tanks and two tank-retrievers. He could not delay. He closed his eyes and drove over the bodies. "I had no choice," Benard kept telling himself as his bulldozer butted through the terraced sand.

By noon the battle for Iwo had risen to a thunderous roar. Amtanks, or "armored pigs" as the Marines called them, still wallowed in the swells offshore to duel with Japanese batteries. Destroyers came in closer and closer and even the mighty battleship *Tennessee* hurled her great shells from a distance of only one mile. But all of this pounding was still not enough to knock down or blow up General Kuribayashi's powerful positions. From Suribachi on the left flank and from the Quarry on the right flank, enemy artillery fire still rained down on the

Marines. Even after they brought in their own artillery, the surest sign that the Americans had come to Iwo Jima to stay, the Marines' counter-battery bombardments could not silence the well-concealed Japanese guns.

At one point, Kuribayashi began to use his highly prized rocket guns. They fired huge missiles varying from 200 to 550 pounds in weight. They were most inaccurate, although it was difficult for them to be harmless while exploding on Iwo's crowded beaches. Still they were largely a failure. They had more bang than bite, passing overhead with a horrible blubbering noise. The Marines nicknamed them "bubbly-wubblies," and soon came to regard them with contempt.

There was no contempt, however, for the Japanese artillery, especially for the guns on that extreme right flank which had so impressed General Cates. Here the Japanese at the Quarry could deliver a plunging fire into the Americans. The Quarry had to be taken, and Colonel Pat Lanigan ordered "Jumpin' Joe" Chambers to do it.

Six feet two inches tall and powerful, Lieutenant Colonel Justice Marion Chambers got his nickname from his bouncy stride. He was a veteran Marine, one of the finest battalion commanders in the corps.

THE TERRIBLE FIRST DAY

At Iwo that day, the men of his battalion were known as "the Ghouls" because of the antiflash cream they wore on their faces.

Jumpin' Joe had noticed high ground commanding the Quarry. He pointed to it and told his officers: "Get up there before those Japs get wise and grab that ground themselves." So up went the Ghouls, their cream no proof against enemy steel. They took the high ground and they finally silenced that dreadful storm of enemy artillery. But they paid for it. By the time Colonel Lanigan was able to relieve Chambers' battalion, it was down from about 1,000 men to 150. Out of one company of 240 Marines only 18 men remained.

That was how the fighting went the first day on Iwo Jima. And that was how General Kuribayashi, who thought he had "allowed" the American Marines to come ashore, found to his dismay that they had come to stay.

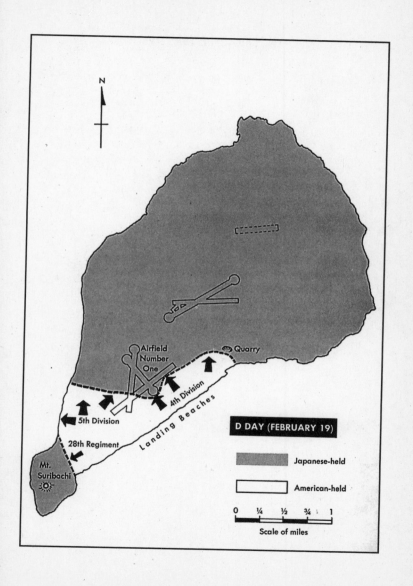

N

Airfield
Number
One

Quarry

4th Division

5th Division

Landing Beaches

28th Regiment

Mt.
Suribachi

D DAY (FEBRUARY 19)

Japanese-held

American-held

0   ¼   ½   ¾   1
Scale of miles

CHAPTER 4

THE FLAG FLIES AT SURIBACHI

THE BATTLE FOR IWO JIMA

By nightfall, the Marines had taken a beachhead 4,000 yards wide from south to north. On the left, where the island had been crossed by men of the 5th Division, the beachhead was 1,000 yards deep. On the right it was only 400 yards deep, or the length of four football fields.

It was an area not half as big as the average Midwestern farm, but it had been seized at a cost of 2,420 killed and wounded Americans. Within the beachhead the carnage was frightful. The sickening stench of death hovered everywhere. Bodies were lying all over. Sometimes the only distinguishing mark between the fallen of both nations was the puttee-tapes on the legs of the Japanese or the yellowish leggings of the Americans. Many of the Japanese dead were naked. Their uniforms had been blasted off them.

Along the beaches the casualties were piling up. Marines coming back for supplies usually brought wounded men with them. They either carried them on stretchers or slung them in ponchos or just helped them hobble to the medical aid stations. Even at the aid stations, the wounded were far from safe. Shells struck these stations repeatedly. On one beach alone, two medical sections, each consisting of a doctor and eight corpsmen, were wiped out. Surgery had to be improvised inside captured Japanese positions. Surgeons smeared with blood worked feverishly through the night, pausing only to smoke or to stretch their aching muscles.

Everyone was cold. Iwo Jima is in the North Pacific and the month was February. Men recently accustomed to tropic heat shivered in temperatures that dropped to 60 degrees. Many wore windbreakers, but their teeth still chattered as they lay on Iwo's cooling sands, bracing for the enemy counterattack they had been told was sure to come. But there was no *banzai* charge. General Kuribayashi did not intend to break his own back with such wasteful tactics. Instead, he kept striking at the invaders with artillery. That was far more effective than any wild suicide rush. All through the night Marines were killed or wounded under steady, relentless Japanese artillery fire. It came blasting into the beachhead from both Suribachi and the northern beachhead. Rockets were also fired, passing overhead with their insane blubber and showers of sparks, rocking the beachhead when they landed. Worst of all was the fire from Suribachi, where the Japanese still looked down the Americans' throats. On the morning of February 20, the Marines on the left flank turned south to attack the volcano.

Colonel Harry Liversedge, a tall, gaunt man known as "Harry the Horse," commanded the 28th Regiment of the 5th Marine Division. The 28th was the outfit assigned to attack Suribachi. Before Harry the Horse and his Marines attacked, Navy and Marine aircraft struck at the volcano. They came roaring in low from the west to hit Suribachi's slopes and base with bombs, rockets and bullets. Tanks of napalm, or jellied gasoline, flashed in great leaping eruptions of flame. Offshore, American warships bombarded the volcano from both flanks. On land, American artillery began to bay with iron voices. Such a thunderous onslaught could not fail to knock out enemy positions. But not enough of them collapsed. The moment the Marines began to advance, they began to suffer casualties. Once again, it was a matter of valor. The Marines had to slog ahead on foot with dynamite and flame throwers, and their net advance for the day was 200 yards.

That night Colonel Kanehiko Atsuchi, the commander of Suribachi, sent up flares to light the American lines for Japanese artillery fire from the north. It came whistling down, and the 28th Marines passed a night nearly as bad as the day. Thus, a dreadful alternating rhythm had begun on Iwo Jima. Every 24 hours was divided into an inferno of

combat by day and a huddled cold hell of enemy
shellfire by night. Each morning the Marines prayed
that they would live to see the dusk; yet the moment
darkness set in, they asked God for the dawn. So
with daylight of February 22, they resumed the
ordeal of assault.

Harry the Horse's regiment was now fully committed, attacking with three battalions abreast. As it
did, a drizzling rain began to fall. Soon it was
pouring. Suribachi's ashes became a sticky gray
paste. It clung to the Marines' clothing and built
platforms of mud under the soles of their shoes. It
fouled their rifle breeches. To eject empty cartridges
the Marines had to work the bolts by hand, thus
slowing their rate of fire. Drenched, mud-smeared,
steadily losing men, Liversedge's regiment punched
down-island to the very base of Suribachi.

They fought all the way. Corporal Dan McCarthy
alone shot 20 Japanese. Sergeant Savage, the Marine
who had helped Tony Stein knock out pillboxes on
D day, killed seven more. Another Marine jumped
into a blockhouse and killed its ten occupants before
he was himself killed. Still another was rushed by
a saber-swinging enemy officer. Seizing the blade
with his bare hands, the Marine wrenched it away.
Then, with dripping hands, he used the sword to kill

the officer. Bunker after bunker was falling. But the Japanese fought back fiercely. Tony Stein was wounded and had to go to the rear.

On the east coast the platoon led by Lieutenant Wells came to an empty enemy pillbox. Sergeant Henry Hansen and Private First Class Donald Ruhl rushed to the top of the position and began exchanging shots with enemy soldiers in a network of trenches behind it. Suddenly, a demolition charge sailed through the air. It landed in front of Hansen and Ruhl.

"Look out, Hank!" Ruhl shouted, and hurled himself on top of the charge to absorb its full blast. The concussion staggered Hansen, spattering him with bits of flesh and blood, and killed Donald Ruhl. This gallant young American had sacrificed his life to save his sergeant.

That was how the Marines fought in the Pacific, and especially on Iwo Jima. Again and again brave young men flung themselves on enemy charges or grenades to save their comrades. They did it instantly, almost without reflection, for they had trained themselves to make the response automatically. With such men, the Marines were unstoppable; and by nightfall the 28th Regiment had battled down to the base of Suribachi and all but surrounded it.

THE FLAG FLIES AT SURIBACHI

By dusk, it was obvious that the Japanese on Suribachi were about ready to crack. Marines could see enemy soldiers leaping to their death from the lip of the crater. This was the Japanese way. To them committing suicide was an honorable end. They were sworn to fight to the death anyway. To die fighting for the divine emperor was the noblest possible end. It meant that their souls would live eternally in Yasakuni Shrine, a mythical hero's heaven similar to the Valhalla of the Norsemen.

Sometimes, though, the Japanese soldiers were in something of a hurry to enter Yasakuni. They had been taught that the Marines were brutal and cruel men who would torture them if they were taken alive. Also, to be taken prisoner was considered disgraceful. Japanese soldiers taken captive against their will or while they were unconscious often pleaded for knives to kill themselves, because, as they explained, they could no longer face their families.

Therefore, whenever the battle began to go against the Japanese, their soldiers began to commit suicide either in order to escape torture or to avoid capture. That certainly did not help the Japanese commander, especially one like Kuribayashi, who had ordered his men "to defend Iwo Jima to the bitter end." It was helpful to the Marines, though.

That night Colonel Liversedge looked grimly at the crater looming darkly above him and said to his officers:

"At dawn we start climbing."

At dawn of February 23, the Americans went up to the top of Suribachi with surprising ease. A patrol consisting of Sergeant Sherman Watson and Privates First Class Ted White, George Mercer and Louis Charlo climbed to the summit without seeing a single enemy soldier. Unknown to them, the surviving Japanese were sitting silently within their caves and caverns.

The patrol returned and reported that the summit of the volcano was undefended. Hearing this, Lieutenant Colonel Chandler Johnson decided to capture it. Colonel Johnson was a stern, pudgy man who impressed his men by roaming the battlefield in full view of the enemy. He didn't wear a helmet and his only weapon was a pistol stuck carelessly in his back pocket. On this momentous Friday morning, Colonel Johnson quickly rounded up a 40-man platoon. Most of the Marines in it had been in Lieutenant Wells's platoon. But Wells had been wounded, and now Lieutenant Harold Schrier was in charge.

"If you reach the top," Johnson said to Schrier, "secure and hold it." He handed the lieutenant a square of colored cloth. "And take this along," he said. The cloth was an American flag. It had been brought ashore from the transport *Missoula*.

Schrier's men began to climb the northern, or inner, slope of Suribachi. Below them, word spread quickly that an attempt was being made to take the high ground that had been such a cruel thorn in the Americans' side. Many Marines paused to watch the patrol's wary ascent. Many men of the invasion fleet were also watching through binoculars.

Tension seemed to mount with each step of that halting ascent. Climbing gingerly, Schrier's men picked their way through the debris of wrecked enemy positions. They could hear the sounds of battle behind them, but up on Suribachi there was only an eerie silence. A half hour after they began to climb, they reached the rim of the crater. They halted. Still silence. Schrier looked around. He could see a few battered enemy emplacements and a few cave entrances. But no Japanese. Silently the lieutenant motioned his men over the rim.

One by one they filed into the crater, fanning out

to take up positions just inside it. Still silence.... One of the Marines tried to provoke the enemy with an insulting gesture. But there was no response. Then, suddenly, a Japanese soldier began climbing out of a deep hole. Corporal Harold Keller fired three times from the hip and the Japanese soldier dropped out of sight. Then hand grenades came flying out of nearby caves. The Marines took cover in the shadows and replied with grenades of their own.

While they did, Corporal Robert Leader and Private First Class Leo Rozek found a flagpole. It was a length of pipe, apparently the remains of a rain-catching system. The flag was affixed to the pipe, which was jammed between rocks, and then Schrier, with Sergeants Henry Hansen and Ernest Thomas, Corporal Charles Lindberg and Private First Class James Michels, raised Old Glory over Iwo Jima. The event was photographed by Sergeant Louis Lowery while Private First Class James Robeson, who refused to get in the picture, stood guard and jeered, "Hollywood Marines!" Thus, at ten-thirty in the morning of February 23, 1945, the Stars and Stripes were flung to the winds whipping over Suribachi.

"There goes the flag!" cried jubilant Marines below. Cheers rose all over the northern end of the island. Some Marines wept in their foxholes. Out on the water the ships of the fleet tootled their whistles in salute. Hospital ships broadcast the news that Suribachi had fallen. For the first time in the war, Japanese soil had been captured by Americans. And when that thrilling small speck of red-white-and-blue broke into view above the gaunt crest of the volcano, even Secretary of the Navy James Forrestal was at hand to see it.

The Secretary had insisted upon coming ashore from the flagship, *Eldorado*. He was standing beside General Holland M. Smith when he saw the symbol of Suribachi's fall. He turned to the general to say: "Holland, the raising of that flag means a Marine Corps for the next 500 years."

On the summit itself, the Japanese had begun to challenge that flag. A rifleman stepped out of a cave and fired at Robeson, who shot him dead with a long burst from his BAR (Browning Automatic Rifle). Then an enemy officer charged out, brandishing a broken sword. A volley of rifle fire tumbled him into the crater. Moving swiftly, the Marines used flame throwers and demolition charges to seal off the summit's caves. Soon other platoons joined them to help mop up the crater.

At the volcano's base, Colonel Johnson became

concerned for his now-famous flag. As he well knew, United States Marines are notorious souvenir hunters. "Some son of a gun is going to want that flag," he said to his adjutant, "but he's not going to get it. That's our flag. Better find another one and get it up there, and bring back ours."

So a runner went looking for a flag. He found a fairly new one, nearly twice as large, aboard Landing Ship 779. As he brought it back to Suribachi, he was accompanied by an Associated Press photographer named Joe Rosenthal.

Rosenthal came panting to the summit of Suribachi in time to photograph the second flag raising. Heaping stones to achieve height, the diminutive Rosenthal hopped up on the pile to take the most famous picture of World War Two. By coincidence, by accident and in haste, he had made the greatest battle photograph of American arms.

Six men helped to put up the second flag. They were: Privates First Class Ira Hayes, Franklin Sousley and Rene Gagnon, Sergeant Michael Strank, Corpsman John Bradley and Corporal Harlon Block. Three of them—Strank, Block and Sousley—were later killed. Bradley was wounded. And of the men who put up the first flag, Sergeants Hansen and Thomas and Private First Class Charlo eventually died on Iwo. Robeson and Michels were wounded.

Thus, five days after the Marines had landed, through valor, sacrifice and in suffering, the United States flag came to fly at Iwo Jima.

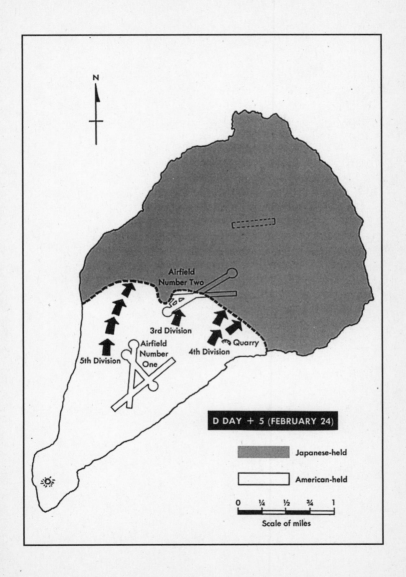

N

Airfield
Number Two

3rd Division

Airfield
Number
One

4th Division

Quarry

5th Division

D DAY + 5 (FEBRUARY 24)

Japanese-held

American-held

0   ¼   ½   ¾   1
Scale of miles

CHAPTER 5

THE UP-ISLAND DRIVE

The capture of Mount Suribachi signaled only the beginning of the battle for Iwo Jima. On Tuesday, the second day of fighting, when Harry the Horse and his 28th Marines had wheeled south against the volcano, the rest of the 5th Division, together with the entire 4th, had faced north for the up-island drive to victory.

It was a nightmare battle. No less than 23 of the men participating would later be awarded the Medal of Honor. In all, the astonishing total of 26 was earned by valor displayed during the fighting on Iwo Jima. One of these was earned by 17-year-old Private First Class Jacklyn Lucas. Standing only 5 feet 8 inches, but weighing 200 pounds, Lucas was a young bull. He was also a "deserter." Eager to see combat, tired of tame duty in a quartermaster shed, he had "joined" the 5th Division by simply going aboard ship when that outfit left Hawaii.

On the first Tuesday morning at Iwo, Lucas and three other Marines were fighting in the 5th's drive up Iwo's west coast. They came to a ravine and were ambushed. Grenades began to fall. One of them dropped among the four Marines. Lucas dove on it. Another came in... Lucas pulled it to him, telling himself: "Luke, you're gonna die." The grenades exploded, but Lucas did not die. Though horribly wounded, and left for dead by the men he had saved, he survived to accept his Medal of Honor.

That same day, on the left, or western, flank Captain Robert Dunlap's company was pinned down while they were attacking a cliff. Dunlap crawled forward through enemy fire to spot the Japanese gun positions. Then he crawled back to relay the information to the artillery and naval gunfire ships. He did this for two days and nights, until the Japanese guns were knocked out and the western beaches were made secure. With these beaches open, supplies could now be unloaded there and thus relieve the congestion on the landing beaches in the east. For his part in this key victory Captain Dunlap won the Medal of Honor.

On the right, or eastern, flank the 5th Division was fighting a fierce battle to overrun Airfield Number One. Throughout the morning, its units were riddled by enemy artillery. Land mines sown in deadly abundance all over the island took a toll of men and tanks. Before the day was over, the Marines were calling for their reserve.

The 21st Regiment of the 3rd Marine Division was ordered to go ashore. Its men were astonished. Calling for the reserve on the *second* day? It had never happened before in all the war. Many of these

Marines had been confident that they would not be called into Iwo. "This one will be over in five days," they said. Even General Schmidt did not believe the conquest of Iwo would take more than ten days.

Yet here, before noon on the second day, the 21st Marines were climbing over the side into their waiting boats. For six hours, in rain and a rough sea, these men circled off Iwo. Then they were ordered back to their transports. They would not come into Iwo until the following day.

Meanwhile, the Marines tried to get more artillery into Iwo. Ducks loaded with heavy 105-millimeter howitzers tried to make it ashore through mounting seas. One after another, eight ducks rolled out of Landing Ship 1032, only to be swamped and sunk by heavy waves. Of twelve guns, only two got safely ashore. Nevertheless, the bigger 155s got in. Landing Ship 779, already famous for being the first to beach at Iwo and for supplying the second flag to fly over Suribachi, came plowing up to the beach. She smashed through the wreckage, swung open her great bow doors—and disgorged four of the heavies on the sand.

The arrival of the 155-millimeter howitzers was an important turning point. These "high-angle fire" guns fired in a looping, up-and-down trajectory.

Thus, they could drop shells on the enemy *behind* his hills, something not possible for the naval guns with their flat line of fire. Moreover, being on land and having their targets pinpointed for them by forward observers, the 155s were also more accurate than bombers. Because of these factors, they were a great help to the Marines as they drove deeper into General Kuribayshi's bristling defenses.

On the third day, the cold rain that had slowed down the Marines moving against Suribachi also bogged down the Marines attacking north. The 4th Division on the right took heavy casualties as its men tried to overrun the high ground along the east coast. Here, Captain Joe McCarthy won a Medal of Honor by charging across open ground to knock out two pillboxes single-handedly. His objective achieved, he called his men forward to occupy a vital ridge.

On the same flank, little Sergeant Ross Gray fought like a one-man battalion. Sergeant Gray was known as "Preacher," because he read his Bible regularly and had once maintained that he could not take another man's life. But when his buddy was killed on Saipan, he changed his mind. On Iwo, Preacher Gray destroyed six pillboxes and killed 25

Japanese soldiers, for which he was awarded the Medal of Honor.

That was how it went on the right flank during that desperate third day, February 21. By nightfall, the 4th Division had lost another 500 men, and the total casualties were up to 2,500.

On the left, the 5th suffered even more grievously. Here the relative flatness of the terrain enabled the Marines to use tanks. Behind these, and supported by shells, rockets and bombs from land, sea and air, the 5th ground out a large gain of 1,000 yards. But it cost 600 men and the 5th's total casualties for the first three days now stood at 2,100

During the day, General Schmidt committed part of the reserve. The 21st Regiment of the 3rd Division came ashore and prepared to go into the center of the line the next day. In the meantime, the Japanese began an aerial counterattack.

Japan had one weapon left to halt the American advance in the Pacific. This was the *kamikaze*. The word means "divine wind," and it commemorates an event immortal in Japanese history. In 1570 the Chinese Emperor assembled a vast fleet to invade Japan. Helpless, the Japanese awaited their doom. But then a *kamikaze* in the shape of a typhoon sprang up to wreck the Chinese fleet and Japan was saved.

In 1944 and 1945 the Japanese leaders made a desperate attempt to save Japan once again, this time from American "invaders." Their strategy was based on the use of suicide pilots, called *kamikaze*. During the battles of Leyte and Luzon, *kamikaze* fliers had appeared in large numbers and, instead of dropping their bombs, they had flown directly into the ships of the American invasion fleet.

At dusk on February 21, fifty *kamikaze* attacked the ships lying off Iwo. Their first victim was the veteran aircraft carrier *Saratoga*. Six planes came plunging down on old "Sara Maru," and two of them crashed in flames near her starboard waterline. A few minutes later another *kamikaze* grazed the *Saratoga*'s flight deck and blew a hold in it before crashing overboard. Nevertheless, *Saratoga* survived the attack. Her fire-fighting crews put out the fires and she began to receive her planes.

Twenty miles east of Iwo Jima the *kamikaze* came upon a circle of six American escort carriers. One of these was the *Bismarck Sea*. A mixture of rain and snow was falling when, at a quarter to seven, a *kamikaze* came boring in on *Bismarck*'s beam. A destroyer saw the plane but withheld fire, believing it to be friendly. It was not, of course, and the suicide plane struck squarely amidships. The stricken ship bucked and quivered. Torpedoes fell from a rack and exploded. Parked airplanes caught fire. Ammunition fell into the flames and began exploding.

At seven o'clock came the order: "Abandon ship!" Over the side, into the cold, black water, dove 800 American sailors and Marines. Down came the Japanese aircraft to strafe them while escort ships rushed to their rescue and fought off their inhuman assailants. Then there was a rocking explosion. *Bismarck Sea*'s stern had blown off, and she rolled over and sank. Lost in the waters around her were 218 Americans.

Three other American ships were also attacked that night, but none was lost. And of the 50 enemy aircraft that had come from Japan in the only successful counterstroke of the Iwo campaign, not one returned to base.

In the early morning darkness of February 22, the 3rd Division entered the fight. Its 21st Regiment relieved the exhausted 23rd of the 4th Division. Now forces advancing up the island consisted of the 5th on the left, the 3rd in the center and the 4th on the right. But the 3rd could make little headway in the center, attacking during a cold rain and under heavy enemy fire. By nightfall they had gained only 250 yards. The men of the 3rd had quickly learned that Iwo Jima was indeed an iron nut of an island to crack.

On the right, meanwhile, the 4th did little more than hold tight. But there were still casualties, and one of them was Jumpin' Joe Chambers. A machine-gun bullet struck him in the left collarbone, piercing his lung and going out his back. As Colonel Chambers lay on the ground receiving medical treatment, Captain Jim Headley came up and tapped him gently on the foot. "Get up you lazy bum," Headley teased. "You were hurt worse on Tulagi." But Jumpin' Joe could not get up this time, and with his evacuation the 25th Regiment had lost all three of the battalion commanders who had landed on D day.

On Friday, February 23, when the flag was raised over Suribachi the news was broadcast to the men attacking to the north.

"Mount Suribachi is ours," a beachmaster blared over his bull horn. "The American flag has been raised over it by the Fifth Marine Division. Fine work, men."

Marines in the north who dared to take their eyes from the front turned to squint to the rear. Some of them saw the flag. But they did not cheer, because *their* objectives still had to be taken. The bull horn might blare again: "We have only a few miles to go to secure this island," but these young Marines knew what they would have to pay for a few miles. "Only," they repeated. "Only..."

In the 3rd Division's central sector the Marines would knock out a bunker or a pillbox and discover that they had ventured into a wicked maze that struck at them from every side. It was just not possible to find a weak spot. The destruction of a single position did not blast a hole which could be widened for a breakthrough. This was because Kuribayashi's defense system was "mutually supporting." An attack on one position not only drew the fire of its guns, but also the massed, converging fire of the other positions around it. Knocking out one position put only one small dent in the enemy's front. It was as though the Japanese had constructed a gigantic Swiss cheese made of steel and concrete. Into this the 3rd Division rammed again and again with very little success.

One company simply could not move. While trying to budge the enemy they had lost eight of their nine flame throwers. The ninth was carried by Corporal Hershel Williams. Covered by four riflemen, Williams attacked. The first yellow burst from his flamer incinerated a Japanese sniper. Next, he destroyed four more enemy soldiers. Moving slowly forward, Williams burned out position after position. In a four-hour assault he destroyed one of the enemy's key networks, and he won the Medal of Honor.

Nevertheless, the center had not moved forward far enough. The 3rd still lagged behind the 5th on the left and the 4th on the right. This prevented the formation of a straight line of attack from coast to coast. The flank divisions did not dare to move ahead for fear of opening gaps between themselves and the 3rd. General Schmidt saw the necessity of straightening the line of attack when he came ashore on the 23rd to take charge of the entire assault. It was also painfully obvious to General Erskine, commander of the 3rd, who had landed on Iwo, too. That night he told his Marines that they must drive forward next day "at all costs."

February 24 was a Saturday. It began with the full weight of American firepower falling on the entrenched, unseen enemy. But the Marines of the

3rd Division had to attack without the benefit of their tanks. Very quickly two company commanders were killed. Lieutenant Raoul Archambault took over one of the companies. A decorated veteran of Bougainville and Guam, the tall, lanky Archambault was an inspiring leader. His men began to yell as he led them forward. Wind-whipped sand pelted their faces like fine buckshot. Yelling louder, the Marines swept through the first line of pillboxes. Then they sprinted up the slopes leading to Airfield Number Two.

Behind Archambault's men the tanks were finally able to come up. They began to clean out the by-passed enemy positions. The Marines were at last punching out that long-desired hole. Now the yelling Americans swept over the airfield. Men in green dungarees fell, but others pressed forward. They rushed up a 50-foot ridge just north of the airfield, and then their own artillery fired on them by mistake. To avoid it, the Marines came back down the hill. The artillery fire stopped and they went up again. Then the Japanese counterattacked and drove them down once more. At this point, another company had come through the hole and joined Archambault's. But both of them were being hit on their exposed flanks and the only way to go was forward.

For the third time, Archambault's men surged up the ridge. As they did, a wave of Japanese soldiers flowed over the crest and came down among them. Brown mingled with green. Hoarse shouts arose in both languages. *"Banzai! Banzai!"* "Kill! Kill!" Standing back to back in ankle-deep sand, fighting with clubbed rifles and bayonets, with knives and fists, the Marines held firm. When the skirmish was over they stood alone among the bodies of 50 dead Japanese. Now the key ridge was theirs, and as they went up again and dug in for the night, the orders to advance "at all costs" were changed to "Hold at all costs."

On that same Saturday the Japanese on the other end of the island received news that Suribachi had been conquered. The report came from one of their naval lieutenants and a party of men he had led through the American lines after their escape from the volcano. But the lieutenant, weary and blood-stained, got a strange reception when he arrived at the headquarters of Captain Samaji Inouye. The captain accused him of leaving his post.

"You traitor!" Captain Inouye bellowed. "Why

did you come here? Don't you know what shame is? You are a coward and a deserter!" Grasping his thick-bladed Samurai saber with both hands, Captain Inouye raised it above his head. "Under military regulations a deserter is executed right away," he shouted. "I shall behead you myself!"

Without a word the lieutenant knelt and bowed his head. He would not argue with a captain. He would not even tell him that he had been ordered to escape. But the blade did not fall. Captain Inouye's aides rushed up to wrest his saber away from him. They knew that the captain believed that every position must be defended to the last man. But they also knew that the lieutenant had escaped to report on Suribachi's fall and to fight again in the north.

Still, Captain Inouye could not restrain his tears. Over and over he murmured, "Suribachi's fallen, Suribachi's fallen." This, he well knew meant the beginning of the end. Thus, the Marines had begun to shake the enemy's belief in their ability to defend Iwo Jima.

Victorious though the Americans might be, they were paying for their progress. After six days of fighting they had lost 1,600 killed, 5,500 wounded and 650 others hospitalized for "combat fatigue," a phrase describing men so shocked or exhausted by battle that they simply cannot go on. In all, the Marines had suffered about 7,750 casualties. Such losses were staggering. With only a little more than a third of Iwo Jima in American possession, the reserve had already gone into action and replacements were being brought ashore to fill out riddled units.

These replacements were not "second-stringers;" they were good, trained men who were the equal of the dead or wounded Marines whose places they took. Instead of being assigned to a regular "outfit," they were part of a big pool of men that each division took along on an invasion. They remained on the ships until they were needed.

Going into battle was doubly hard on replacements. They had no friends, because the squads they had trained in had been broken up so that the men could be fed piecemeal into the units already engaged. Replacements were the waifs of war. They joined a squad as perfect strangers and, as often happens, the "dirty duty" fell to them. A group of replacements arriving at the headquarters of a battle formation might receive a greeting like this: "Okay, you men are in F Company now. In a couple of minutes we're going to be moving out. So remember this: keep both ends down, your heads and your tails, and don't shoot no Marines."

With that, the replacements entered their baptism of fire. Once they had survived a day or two of it, however, they came to be regarded as "good Marines" and were accepted into their squads with all the comradeship accorded any "original." Actually, on Iwo Jima it was a rare squad that survived with most of its originals. By the time the battle was over, the "boot" replacements had become the "old salts."

As the replacements went into line on February 25, the seventh day of battle, the last of the reserve was also committed. These men were the 9th Marines of the 3rd Division. The 9th relieved the 21st in the center. It moved through the small hole punched in the enemy line by Archambault's men, and went slugging with an agonizing slowness toward Hill 199.

This hill was vital. It commanded Airfield Number Two. And the enemy there held out for three days. A major factor in the capture of the hill was the one-man battle fought by Private First Class Wilson Watson. After destroying a pillbox single-handed, Watson climbed a ridge and stood boldly outlined against the sky while killing 60 Japanese with his automatic rifle. He came down only after he ran out of ammunition, and many Marines believed that it was a miracle that Wilson Watson lived to receive his Medal of Honor.

When Hill 199 passed into American hands on February 27, the uneven Marine line was at last straightened out. All but a few yards of Airfield Number Two had been captured and roughly one third of Iwo Jima was not conquered. Some 50,000 Americans were ashore and 2,000 of them were Seabees already at work expanding and improving Airfield Number One. Beneath the rising and falling roar of battle there now ran the steady growling of the bulldozers. Not all of them, of course, were at work on the airfields.

Some of them were building cemeteries.

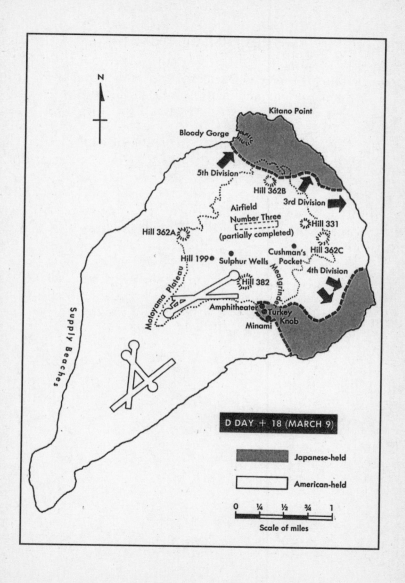

N

Kitano Point

Bloody Gorge

5th Division

Hill 362B

3rd Division

Airfield
Number Three
(partially completed)

Hill 331

Hill 362A

Cushman's
Pocket

Hill 362C

Hill 199   Sulphur Wells

4th Division

Motoyama Plateau

Hill 382

Meatgrinder

Amphitheater   Turkey
Knob

Minami

Supply Beaches

D DAY + 18 (MARCH 9)

Japanese-held

American-held

0   ¼   ½   ¾   1

Scale of miles

An enemy cave gives shelter to a doctor
and corpsmen administering first aid.
Courtesy USMC

Marines advance on Japanese positions as a mortar shell explodes in front of their supporting tank. They gained a total of 20 yards with a loss of 30 men.
Courtesy USMC

A marine fires on a Japanese soldier
he has just spotted.
Courtesy USMC

Men of the 3rd battalion, 28th Regiment, make a direct frontal attack over the top of a rocky bridge. *Courtesy USMC*

The most famous battle photograph of World War II
was this, the second flag raising on Mt. Suribachi
taken by Associated Press photographer Joe Rosenthal.
Courtesy USMC

Lieutenant Schrier's men blow up an enemy cave
entrance after raising the first flag on Mt. Suribachi.
The smoke coming from both sides of the ridge
shows that this cave had two entrances.
Courtesy USMC

Major General Rockey directs the 5th Division
from his command post.
Courtesy USMC

The crew of a 155-millimeter howitzer flinch
as their gun recoils from the blast.
Courtesy USMC

Major General Erskine gives orders to his officers at the
3rd Division's command post near Airfield Number One.
Courtesy USMC

These two men are preparing "pole charges" from blocks of TNT. The charges are thrust into the entrances to enemy positions and then detonated.
Courtesy USMC

Forward observers correct artillery fire from
a shell crater near Airfield Number Two. A wrecked
Japanese plane provides concealment.
Courtesy USMC

Replacements await assignment on
Iwo's cluttered beaches.
Courtesy USMC

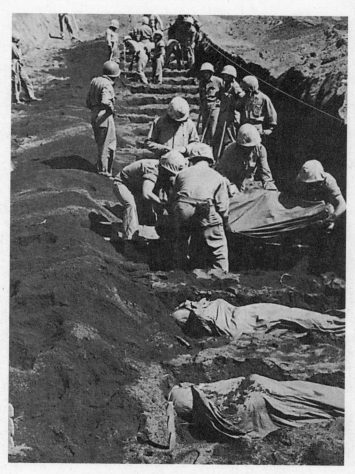

Burial detail places bodies of fallen Marines
in grave trenches dug by Seabees.
Courtesy USMC

Dinah Might, crippled in a raid on Japan, approaches Airfield Number one to make the first emergency landing on Iwo Jima.
Courtesy USAF

A flame-throwing tank pours a stream of
burning oil into an enemy strongpoint.
Courtesy USMC

A Japanese soldier emerges from his cave after listening
to a surrender appeal. The majority of the enemy,
however, chose to fight to the death.
Courtesy USMC

CHAPTER 6

INTO THE MEATGRINDER

On February 25, two days before the fall of Hill 199, the American attack on both flanks had begun to grind down to a bloody crawl. On the west coast, the 5th Division had come up against a system of fortified ridges crowned by the bastion known as Hill 362A. On the east coast the 4th had entered the "Meatgrinder."

The Meatgrinder was the name which the Marines had given to a defensive system lying roughly halfway up the island, just east of airfield Number Two. Here they were quite literally torn apart on the Meatgrinder's three cruel blades. These were Hill 382, the highest ground on northern Iwo; a little bald hill known as Turkey Knob; and a rocky bowl called the Amphitheater. Within this complex lay the Japanese communications system. Here, unseen among a network of caves and tunnels, the Japanese had kept the Marines under observation since D day.

The approach to the Meatgrinder offered no concealment. Bombardment from every quarter had stripped the area of its oak trees and laid bare a maze of rocks and brush criscrossed by defiles running to the sea. All the approaches were covered by tanks buried up to their gun turrets. Behind them, cleverly concealed or out of sight in the caves, were machine guns and mortars, antitank guns, and light artillery and antiaircraft guns depressed to fire point-blank. Hill 382, Turkey Knob and the Amphitheater were also mutually supporting. They could defend themselves or one another. It was not possible to take the Meatgrinder point by point, but only by laying all three points under attack at once.

The 4th Marine Division began its assault with a furious bombardment. Land artillery thundered, naval gunfire bellowed, mortar boats and landing ships ran in close to the shoreline to fire up the defiles. While bobbing amtanks put the coastal flank under fire, carrier aircraft came screaming down through the smoke and dust to strafe and bomb. As the bombardment rose in fury, the 4th tried to get around to the enemy's rear by sending its tanks on a sweep through the 3rd Division's area. Meanwhile, armored tankdozers butted paths through a rubble of smashed rocks.

Then the foot troops attacked. At first, the Marines went up Hill 382 with surprising ease. But once they reached the summit, the enemy recovered from the shock of the bombardment and opened fire. The Marines were pinned to the ground. They were even struck from the rear, where they had unknowingly passed a hidden system of pillboxes. Under cover of a smoke screen, the Marines came down from Hill 382. The day's gains were 100 yards, or "one touchdown," as Major Frank Garretson would say. This former football star was fond of measuring advances on Iwo in terms of 100-yard "touchdowns."

With the close of battle that night, the Marines held about two-fifths of Iwo Jima and had suffered 8,000 casualties since landing. In Japan, a jubilant but not exactly truthful Radio Tokyo broadcast reports of wholesale slaughter of the Americans. The enemy's hold on Iwo Jima, the broadcast declared, was "not more than the size of the forehead of a cat." Many Marines in front of Hill 382 would have agreed with that estimate, at least as far as their own area was concerned. They did not realize that they were assaulting the eastern half of General Kuribayashi's main line of defense. Even a gain of "one touchdown" was more than the Japanese commander was willing to surrender.

A touchdown was about all the Marines got on the following day, February 26. But they did knock out the pillbox positions they had by-passed. This was done by Private First Class Douglas Jacobson, a rifleman. As he started toward Hill 382 again that day, he saw an American bazooka man go down.

Jacobson dropped his rifle and seized the bazooka. Running from position to position like a man berserk, he destroyed 16 pillboxes, knocked out a tank and killed 75 Japanese soldiers. Much of his regiment's advance that day was due to Jacobson, who received a Medal of Honor for his valor. Yet the Marines had to withdraw for the night.

The same sort of thing was happening at Turkey Knob and the Amphitheater. Every time the Marines drove deep into the enemy defenses, they were made to pay dearly for it. The Japanese simply pulled back and called down the mortar and artillery fire which had been "zeroed-in" on their own positions. After the Americans were forced out at dusk, the Japanese returned to prepare a bloody encore for the following day.

For one full week—from February 25 to March 3—the 4th Marine Division was ground to a bloody pulp in the Meatgrinder. Casualties rose at such an alarming rate that the 4th used 400 pints of fresh blood on a single day. Yet each day's assault left Kuribayashi's eastern anchor weaker and weaker. General Cates fed more and more fresh units into the battle. One by one, the Japanese positions were blasted to rubble or sealed off.

At Turkey Knob a 75-millimeter howitzer was

dragged over rock and rubble to deliver point-blank fire at a blockhouse that was the center of the height's defenses. Under covering rifle fire, demolition men crawled up to the blockhouse walls. They planted their charges to tear gaping holes in the walls. Then tankdozers cut a path through the rubble for a flamethrowing tank. Rumbling forward with its flame thrower hissing, the tank poured streams of flame through the holes. Still the blockhouse held out. So did Turkey Knob, so did the Amphitheater, so did Hill 382.

On Friday, March 2, after six days of assault on the Meatgrinder, the 4th Marine Division hit this wicked trio with all its strength. Turkey Knob and the Amphitheater were each attacked by a regiment. The objective was to prevent these strongpoints from firing on the force attacking Hill 382. In this, the Marines were successful.

Company E, under Major Rolo and Carey, and Company F, under Captain Walter Ridlon, prepared to move out against Hill 382. Before they did, heavy artillery laid down a barrage. Supporting fire from tanks and whooshing flights of missiles launched by rocket trucks also helped. Major Carey's men attacked on the left, Captain Ridlon's on the right. By mid-morning one of Carey's platoons was just under the smashed radar antenna, which was situated atop the hill.

Then Carey was cut down by machine-gun fire. Captain Pat Donlan took over E Company. A few hours later Donlan was hit by shrapnel. First Lieutenant Stanley Osborne replaced him, only to be killed by a shellburst, which tore off Donlan's right leg at the same time while killing one more officer and wounding another. Now Second Lieutenant Richard Reich was the only officer left in this riddled company.

Meanwhile, Captain Ridlon's F Company was advancing. Running into far less fire, the Marines here on the right worked quickly up beneath the crest of the hill. Then they took it with a rush, and at mid-afternoon, Captain Ridlon radioed headquarters that he was on top of Hill 382. That night Major Garretson wrote in his diary: "Day's progress, a little over two touchdowns." Although the Marines held the top of the hill, they had not yet conquered it. And on the following day E Company passed through another ordeal.

First Lieutenant William Crecink had replaced Lieutenant Reich as its commander, but he was quickly wounded and Reich took over again. Then Captain Charles Ireland relieved him, only to be wounded. For a third time, Reich led E Company. For a third time he was relieved, by Captain Robert O'Mealia. But Captain O'Mealia was killed by a shellburst. For Lieutenant Reich, however, there was no fourth term at command of E Company. That was because there was no longer any E Company.

What remained of it was joined with Captain Ridlon's riddled F Company. With this patched-up force, Ridlon cleaned out Hill 382's last defenders. Turkey Knob and the Amphitheater still sputtered in defiance, but only weakly. On the following day they were safely by-passed to be reduced at leisure later. The dreadful Meatgrinder had been shattered and Kuribayashi's first line of defense penetrated.

Again the cost had been high. The 4th Division had suffered 2,880 casualties during the week-long battle at the Meatgrinder. Now its total losses on Iwo were 6,600 men killed and wounded.

In the center, meanwhile, the 3rd Division was also piercing Kuribayashi's first line of defense, punching through in a series of slanting attacks and overrunning the half-completed Airfield Number Three.

On the left, however, the 5th Division was passing through an ordeal only a little less fierce than the 4th's.

INTO THE MEATGRINDER

The 5th Division's up-island drive had freed the western beaches, where, despite a high and treacherous surf, a second supply line to the fighting front was being built. General Harry Schmidt had located his Fifth Corps headquarters there, and on March 1 he was joined by "Howlin' Mad" Smith. As the two men talked outside Schmidt's tent, they noticed that the ammunition ship *Columbia Victory* had moved inshore to unload shells.

Suddenly Japanese artillery began shelling her! Shell after shell came screaming down from enemy-held high ground. The two Marine generals exchanged glances of consternation. They both knew that a direct hit on the *Columbia Victory* would detonate her thousands of tons of ammunition, which would probably wreck lower Iwo Jima with all its men and supplies.

As they watched, the first two salvos fell astern of *Columbia Victory*. The ammunition ship turned and ran for the open sea. Then a third salvo fell ahead of the vessel. The generals tensed. So did everyone on the beach. "The next one's going to hit her square," said Smith.

But the fourth salvo missed, dropping in the water astern. Before more artillery could fire, *Columbia Victory* was safely out of range. She would not return until the Marines battling westward across the ridges could silence the enemy's guns.

Hill 362A fell on the same day. But the gallant corporal Tony Stein lost his life while helping to reduce that strongpoint. His captain had asked for volunteers for patrol, and Tough Tony Stein had volunteered. He did not return. Three of the men who helped to raise flags over Suribachi also died during the 5th's conquest of Hill 362A. So did Lieutenant Colonel Chandler Johnson, the battalion commander who had ordered the Stars and Stripes unfurled atop the volcano. And Gunnery Sergeant William Walsh won the Medal of Honor on Hill 362A, when he gallantly smothered an enemy explosive with his body to save his men.

Hill 362A, just 20 feet lower than Hill 382 on the east coast, had been almost as fiercely defended. Sometimes the Marines burned the Japanese out of their caves by rolling gasoline drums inside and shooting them alight. At other times they hung from the cliff ledges to lower explosives into the caves on ropes.

True to their word, the brave Japanese defending the hill had fought to the last man. True to the strange Japanese tradition of suicide, the lone survivor killed himself. Marines watched cautiously as he crept out of a cave with a grenade in his hand. They ducked behind a rock when he tapped it on his helmet to arm it. But it did not go off, and when the Marines lifted their heads again they saw that the Japanese had the grenade held to his ear as though listening to it. He tapped it again, and listened. No explosion. A third time.... It went off.

The fall of Hill 362A did not halt the 5th's advance. The division continued to sweep forward, driving toward the northern coast. On March 3, the 5th was staggered by its losses of 518 killed and wounded, its second worst casualty day during the entire campaign. But on that day five of the Division's men won Medals of Honor, an amazing record in American military history.

Corporal Charles Berry and Private First Class William Caddy won their Medals by laying down their lives for their comrades. Both of them leaped on sputtering enemy grenades.

Medical corpsman George Wahlen lived to receive his Medal, although he was wounded three times in six days. His last wound was very serious, but Wahlen insisted on accompanying the Marines to treat the wounded. At last, however, he collapsed and had to be evacuated.

Sergeant William Harrell was on sentry duty early

that morning when an enemy grenade sailed in on him. It exploded, breaking his thigh bone and tearing off his left hand. Then a Japanese attacked, brandishing a saber. Drawing his pistol with his right hand, Harrell shot him dead. More Japanese attacked. Harrell fought them off until he sank to the ground from loss of blood. A Japanese then ran up and put a grenade under his head. Harrell killed him and pushed the grenade as far from himself as he could. When it exploded, it killed another Japanese and tore off Harrell's right hand. With that the Marine sergeant lost consciousness. He was found at dawn lying senseless among a dozen dead Japanese. He had held his position, and he would live to receive his nation's highest award.

Corpsman Jack Williams won the fifth Medal of Honor that day. During a grenade battle he ran out in the middle ground to treat a wounded Marine. As he knelt over the stricken man, a sniper shot him three times. Still, Williams worked on. Only after he had finished treating the Marine did he turn to bind up his own perforated belly. Next he gave first aid to a second Marine. But then an enemy bullet cut him down for good.

With such men General Keller Rockey's battling 5th at last punched though the western anchor of

Kuribayashi's strongest line. The 5th's advance, combined with the conquest of the Meatgrinder in the east and the 3rd Division's penetration in the center, meant that defeat was overtaking the enemy.

By March 3, thirteen days after D day, General Kuribayashi had lost most of his artillery and his tanks, along with 65 per cent of his officers. He had only 3,500 front-line troops able to fight. His communications had been shattered. This meant that he could not contact his subordinate commanders in charge of the different sectors of defense. As a result, the Japanese force defending Iwo was like a body fighting without its head.

Still General Kuribayashi was determined to fight on. He radioed Tokyo: "I am not afraid of the fighting power of only three American Marine divisions, if there are no bombardments from aircraft and warships."

However, the American bombardments were continuous. But in spite of them, the Japanese commander had managed to inflict the worst casualties of the war on the attacking Marines. During two terrible weeks the Americans had lost 3,000 killed and 13,000 wounded. They did not know yet that they had cracked through the enemy's strongest defenses. All that they could see was that nearly half the island was still in Japanese hands.

CHAPTER 7

BREAKTHROUGH

Now that the Americans had taken more than half of Iwo Jima they discovered that "Sulphur Island" was indeed as strange as it was ugly.

At the southern end of the island and around the airfields, Marines still shivered in their foxholes at night. But farther north they had come to the Japanese sulphur wells. Here, General Smith said, "it looked like something left over when they finished building Hell."

The air was foul with the smell of sulphur. Sulphur mists rising to the surface had stained the earth dead white and pale yellow. Marines could scarcely dig a foxhole without starting a sulphur bath. They could cook a can of C rations by burying it in the earth for a quarter-hour. When they wanted to make coffee, they took their canteens to the sulphur wells. Sometimes the temperature of the water rising to the surface was 160 or 170 degrees.

As usual, the Marines took oddities like these in their stride. They had fought and won campaigns in the malarial swamps and jungles of the Solomons, and on the blistering-hot coral atolls of the Gilberts and Marshalls and Carolines. They knew that they would do the same on this peculiar, cold-hot hump of sand and rock. On March 4, it appeared that General Kuribayashi was inclined to agree with them. On that day he radioed Tokyo asking for aircraft and warships to come to his aid. "Send me these things," he said, "and I will hold this island. Without them I cannot hold."

As the Japanese commander might have suspected, he was not to get either planes or ships, However, on that very same day, his enemy received a wonderful boost for *their* morale.

During the afternoon of March 4, Radioman William Welsh was monitoring the air-sea rescue frequency aboard the command ship *Auburn*. He had just finished a crossword puzzle when the loudspeaker overhead suddenly came to life:

"Hello Gatepost, this is Nine Bakecable. We are lost. Give us a bearing."

"Hello Nine Bakecable, this is Gatepost," Welsh replied. "Who are you?"

"We are a monster short on fuel. Give us instructions please."

An officer checked a list of code names and discovered that a "monster" was a B-29. The Superforts had raided Japan only that morning. Obviously, one of the giant bombers was asking for permission to make an emergency landing on Iwo Jima! Excitement ran like an electric shock through the *Auburn*. At once, aerial transports from the Marianas were warned to keep away from Iwo. Ashore, the emergency field was cleared for the landing of a "big one."

No more than two weeks after the Marines had first landed on Iwo, the island was beginning to serve its purpose—even with a savage struggle for the island still going on. As the word spread across Iwo, Marines, soldiers and Seabees came running toward the airfield.

Out over the ocean, the B-29 *Dinah Might* flew through the rain and mist with open bomb-bay doors. That was *Dinah Might*'s trouble. The doors would not close, and the wind whistling through the opening had slowed the plane and forced it to consume most of its fuel. When Lieutenant Fred Malo, the pilot, tried to tap the spare tanks he found that the valve would not open. For *Dinah Might* it was Iwo or the Ocean.

Now Sergeant James Cox, *Dinah Might*'s radioman, was getting a bearing from *Auburn*. "Course 167 for 28 miles," Welsh instructed him. "Do you prefer to ditch offshore or try to land on the strip?"

"We prefer to land."

"Roger. We will have the field cleared for you."

Soon Lieutenant Malo sighted Iwo Jima. It was a tiny speck in the sea, growing to cinder size, then larger... larger.... Twice Malo circled the island. Each time the narrow runway slid out of sight. On the third pass he hit the runway squarely. The 60-ton aircraft whacked the matting with a *whhhumphf!* like an exploding shell. Then it was whizzing between lanes of wildly cheering Americans, its left wing cutting down a telephone pole like a sickle slicing straw, its roaring motors whipping up a huge cloud of dust. When the dust settled, *Dinah Might* stood safely at the end of the runway. Lieutenant Malo and his men were the first of many B-29 crews to land on Iwo. A total of 2,251 Superforts, carrying 24,61 Americans, were saved by emergency landings on this tiny island.

That was the value of Iwo. And for the first time during the war, the value of an objective had been made evident even before it was taken.

The day after *Dinah Might*'s dramatic landing, the Marines on Iwo Jima rested. General Schmidt gave his tired men a "day off." They read letters, ate hot "chow," and where possible they scrubbed Iwo's gritty gray grime off their bodies or treated themselves to the luxury of a shave. In the meantime, the divisions reorganized. Generals Schmidt and Smith had decided on a coordinated attack the next day by all three divisions. This, they hoped, would break through Kuribayashi's last line and bring a quick victory.

The quest for quick victory had brought the Marines back to the assault again and again. The sooner the island was won the sooner the invasion fleet could be released for duty elsewhere. Victory would gain more airfields to provide fighter cover for the B-29s bombing Japan. It would provide flank cover for the invasion of Okinawa, thus speeding up the timetable of conquest.

In wartime the attempt to achieve a quick victory may seem a needless sacrifice of lives, but in the long run it saves lives. The rapid conquest of lower Iwo Jima with its big airfield had already begun to save American airmen and their valuable B-29s.

So on the morning of March 6 the heaviest bombardment of the campaign was begun. It was devastating. All the guns ashore and at sea blasted away. In 67 minutes the Marines fired 22,500 shells of all sizes at the enemy positions. A battleship and two cruisers added 50 rounds of huge 14-inchers and 400 rounds of 5-inch shells. Three destroyers and two landing ships also opened up, and from the carriers came aircraft dropping bombs and tanks of napalm. It did not seem that the enemy could survive such a rain from the sky.

But they did. When the Marines rose up to attack, they were met by a dreadful hail of enemy fire. Once again they were forced to close in and chase the enemy down his warrens of rock and concrete, along his underground burrows and right into his formidable blockhouses. The Japanese were simply not going to be blasted into defeat.

While the Marines were struggling to make some more headway, the Army Air Corps began to arrive on the island. Twenty-eight P-51 Mustang fighters and twelve P-61 Black Widow night fighters roared into Iwo. For the second time, the value of quick victory had been demonstrated.

That night, however, the advance was still being measured in bloody "touchdowns."

The failure of the artillery barrage had convinced General Erskine of the 3rd Division that the enemy had to be surprised, not overwhelmed. Erskine realized that the Japanese had skillfully adapted themselves to American assault. When artillery began the onslaught preceding each day's attack, the enemy soldiers merely ran down into their deepest underground positions to sit out the bombardment. When the fire lifted, they ran back up to their guns to greet the advancing Marines with shot and shell. They had done it so often that they could now do it with split-second timing. As a result, the barrages were next to worthless.

General Erskine's solution was a surprise predawn attack without artillery. His division still held the center, and its mission was to crack straight through to the other end of the island. When that was accomplished, the Japanese would be split in two. Then the 4th Division on the right would clean out all resistance in its area, while the 3rd would join the 5th in mopping up the left.

Blocking the 3rd Division's path to the sea was a height called 362C. This hill covered other Japanese positions on the right. (All of these enemy positions were located on the high ground of Motoyama Plateau.) So General Erskine ordered one battalion to take Hill 362C by surprise attack, while two other battalions slipped into position to attack the enemy emplacements on the right. (All of these enemy positions were located on the high ground of Motoyama Plateau.) So General Erskine ordered one battalion to take Hill 362C by surprise attack, while two other battalions slipped into position to attack the enemy emplacements on the right. Once Hill 362C was taken and its guns silenced, the two battalions on the right could begin to attack without fear of flanking fire.

At five o'clock in the morning, with a whistling wind hurling cold rain in their faces, the Marines moved out. Not a shot was fired. Not a hand was raised against them. The two battalions in the center and right reported having moved 200 yards. On the left at Hill 362C, the Marines came upon the Japanese asleep in their trenches and killed all of them. Jubilant, they reported that they had taken Hill 362C.

But they had not!

By mistake they had climbed and conquered Hill 331. At daylight Hill 362C began to pour fire onto the center and right battalions, pinning them down. Now a desperate battle began. Throughout the day the trapped Marine battalions fought back. But their number was steadily whittled.

In the center, 200-man companies were down to barely more than 10-man squads. By nightfall, Lieutenant Wilcie O'Bannon commanded fewer than 10 men in F Company. They were huddled on a mound 300 yards inside the Japanese strongpoint. After O'Bannon's radio fell silent, Lieutenant Colonel Robert Cushman ordered tanks to the rescue. Thirty-six hours after the predawn attack began, the tanks rumbled up to the mound where O'Bannon lay with just four men. Straddling the Marines, the tankers reached through the escape hatches in the bellies of the tanks and dragged them safely inside. Company E under Captain Maynard Schmidt in the same sector fared only slightly better: it had seven survivors.

To the right, other companies were being cut up by enemy fire. Here Lieutenant John Leims risked death three times to save his Marines. He crawled 400 yards through enemy fire to lay communications wire from his cut-off company to battalion headquarters. Then he withdrew the company, after which he twice crawled back to his abandoned position to rescue wounded Marines there. For this, Lieutenant Leims received the Medal of Honor.

So did Lieutenant Jack Lummus, who was fighting with the 5th Division just a little to the left of the embattled 3rd. Lieutenant Lummus was a former All-America end at Baylor University. Now, instead of carrying him on a touchdown run, his powerful legs were carrying him out in front of his pinned-down company. A grenade knocked Lummus sprawling, but he jumped up and rushed on, knocking out a gun emplacement. Another grenade downed him, shattering his shoulder. He arose and dashed forward, again destroying an enemy position and killing its defenders.

Lieutenant Lummus then turned and called to his men to follow him. Inspired by his courage and leadership, they arose and charged, pouring through the enemy network. Then a land mine exploded with a roar and a shower of dirt. When the smoke cleared Jack Lummus appeared to be standing in a hole. The explosion had torn off both legs and he was standing on the bloody stumps, still urging his men forward.

They ran to him sobbing. Some Marines wanted to end his agony for him, but he motioned them forward. As they went, their tears turned to rage and they killed and blasted all before them. At the end of the day they were on a ridge over looking the sea.

To their rear, Jack Lummus lay in the division hospital. Pint after pint of blood was fed into his veins. He received 18 pints in all, but the doctors and Lummus knew that it was hopeless. Yet, as the lieutenant's immense vitality slowly left him, his gaiety remained. "Doc," he said at the end, "it looks like the New York Giants have lost a darn good end." With his remaining strength he smiled, and then he died.

So it went throughout that tragic March 7. In spite of all their losses, however, the Marines had not suffered disaster. In the 3rd Division's sector, the battalion that had taken the wrong hill finally fought forward to Hill 362C. In the center and on the right, the sector now known as "Cushman's Pocket" still resisted hotly and eight more days of fighting would be required to subdue it. But, as company after company entered the battle, Japanese resistance on Motoyama Plateau waned and finally died. By nightfall of March 7, the valuable high ground of the plateau was in Marine hands, and the end was in sight.

The enemy also seemed to believe that the end was near. As on Suribachi to the south, the Japanese in the north had begun to kill themselves. On that bloody March 7, a hundred enemy soldiers who were holed up inside a ridge on the left flank blew themselves up. But they also took with them a good part of a company of Marines atop the ridge.

With nightfall of March 8 there came the second proof of Japanese despair: the *banzai* charge.

This one was led by Captain Inouye, who was still grieving over the loss of Suribachi. He wanted to recapture the volcano and to wreck the American aircraft parked on Airfield Number One. To do so he would have to break through the 4th Division on his left flank. In all, he gathered about 1,000 men of his naval force. Most of them had rifles or grenades, but some had only bamboo spears. Many more had wound explosives around their waists. These human bombs planned to hurl themselves against American equipment.

Just before midnight, they started south. They did not charge immediately. Instead they crawled stealthily forward, hoping to slip through the American lines. But the moment they were detected, they arose and with turkey-gobbler shrieks of *"Banzai! Banzai!"* they came swarming forward.

Up went the Marine flares. Down came the Navy's star shells. In that flickering, ghastly, artificial light, Marine mortars crumped and thumped among the charging enemy. Marine machine-gun fire cut them down and popping rifles picked them off. The battle was very quickly over, although, as in most night battles, sporadic firing continued until dawn. Daylight disclosed 784 enemy dead. Although the Marines had lost 90 killed and 257 wounded, Captain Inouye's *banzai* had been their biggest break so far.

That afternoon the Marines received the welcome news that the other end of the island had been reached. Under Lieutenant Paul Connally, a 28-man platoon from the 3rd Division came to a high bluff. Looking down, they saw the ocean. Scrambling below in full view of dumfounded enemy gunners, they waded into the water and scooped it up to wash the grit of Iwo from their faces. Some men took off their shoes to bathe their feet. But then the enemy gunners recovered from their surprise and began firing. Men fell, wounded, and the patrol withdrew. Some of the men returned, however, to fill a canteen with salt water to prove that the 3rd Division had been the first to traverse the length of Iwo. The canteen was sent back to General Erskine with the warning: "For inspection, not consumption."

Eighteen days after the battle for Iwo Jima began, the island had been traversed. What was left of the defenders had been cut in two, and now the pieces had to be destroyed.

CHAPTER 8

'TILL THE LAST MAN

The night that the Marine patrol reached the sea, General Tadamichi Kuribayashi gave Tokyo its first hint of approaching defeat.

All surviving units have suffered heavy losses," he declared in a message. "I am very sorry that I have let the enemy occupy one part of Japanese territory, but I am taking comfort in giving him heavy losses."

The general and his men were indeed doing just that. Even though only about 1,500 Japanese soldiers remained, they were still fighting stubbornly. On the right, where General Cates's 4th Division was fighting, there were numerous enemy pockets still holding out. Here General Cates tried to reach Major General Sadusi Senda, commander of the Japanese 2nd Mixed Brigade, which opposed the 4th. He prepared a surrender appeal which said:

"You have fought a gallant and heroic fight, but you must realize Iwo Jima has been lost to you. You can gain nothing by further resistance, nor is there any reason to die when you can honorably surrender and live to render valuable service to your country in the future. I promise and guarantee you and the members of your staff the best of treatment. I respectfully request that you accept my terms of honorable surrender."

It is not known if General Senda ever received this message. Nor was his body ever found when, on March 16, the 4th turned from killing enemy soldiers to counting their corpses. On that date all resistance on the right, or eastern, flank ended. Three days later, the battered, riddled 4th took ship for Hawaii. It had suffered 9,098 casualties on Iwo Jima, and 1,806 of these men were buried there. In just 14 months, the 4th Marine Division had fought three major battles and had suffered 17,722 casualties. So the 4th sailed away from that black, bloody curse of an island, never to enter combat again in World War Two.

On the left, however, the 5th and 3rd were still in battle. Here the remaining enemy soldiers were under the command of Colonel Masuo Ikeda. They were pressed into a square mile of tumbled ravines and gorges. One of these, about 700 yards long and from 200 to 300 yards wide, became the scene of Kuribayashi's last stand. It was at first impossible to use tanks or other vehicles, and the savagery of the fighting gave the area the name of "Bloody Gorge."

On March 13 a Marine patrol came very close to capturing General Kuribayashi in a cave within the Gorge. The Americans peered into the cave and the general's orderly quickly blew out the candles and wrapped his chief in a blanket. Some of the Marines ventured inside. They paused, peered around, and then departed—and the heart of the general's orderly ceased its mad pounding.

Next day Bloody Gorge shrank still smaller. On that day, Private Franklin Sigler led a charge against the gun position which had barred his company's advance for several days. He reached it unhurt, knocked it out and killed its crew. Immediately, enemy fire came plunging down on him from Japanese caves and tunnels. Sigler responded by scaling the rocks and destroying these positions as well. But he was seriously wounded in the skirmish. Still, he refused evacuation and continued to direct American fire into the Japanese positions. Under fire he also carried three wounded comrades to safety, and he went to the rear himself only when ordered to do so. Sigler won the Medal of Honor for his actions, which played a large part in the destruction of the defenders of the Gorge—Japan's famous 145th Infantry Regiment.

Kuribayashi's concern now was for the 145th's regimental flag. In the Japanese army a unit's colors were sacred. If they were ever lost, the unit's name was stricken from the army rolls in disgrace.

Japanese officers very readily sacrificed their lives for their colors, and to be named to the color guard was the highest honor which could befall a Japanese soldier. Because of this, General Kuribayashi asked Colonel Ikeda how much longer the regimental flag would be safe.

"Maybe a day," the colonel replied, and Kuribayashi said: "Burn it. Do not let it fall into the hands of the enemy." Ikeda obeyed, reporting from his command post: "Here we burnt our brilliant regimental flag completely. Good-by."

A few days later, General Erskine attempted to persuade Colonel Ikeda to surrender. His appeal said: "The fearlessness and indomitable fighting spirit which has been displayed by the Japanese troops on Iwo Jima warrants the admiration of all fighting men. You have handled your troops in a superb manner, but we have no desire to annihilate brave troops who have been forced into a hopeless position. Accordingly, I suggest that you cease resistance at once and march, with your command, through my lines to a place of safety where you and your officers and men will be humanely treated in accordance with the rules of war."

General Erskine sent the message in care of two captured Japanese soldiers. One of them reached

Ikeda's cave. He sent the message inside by a friend, and then, becoming frightened, he ran back to the Marine lines. There was no reply from Colonel Ikeda. The 5th Division would have to clean out the enemy hornet's nest in the Bloody Gorge.

It was grim work. Powdered gray with the dust of Iwo, their dungarees cut to rags and tatters by the rocky terrain that they traversed, General Rockey's Marines moved relentlessly from point to point. At last they came to a huge blockhouse at the southeast corner of the Gorge. It was the last Japanese position standing above ground on Iwo, and it supposedly stood above Kuribayashi's headquarters. Again and again the Marines struck at it with shellfire and 40-pound shaped demolition charges. But the blockhouse was too strong and did not fall. Finally, the Marines by-passed it and began to knock out its supporting positions.

By March 16, Tadamichi Kuribayashi knew that the end had come. That morning he instructed his officers and men to sally forth at midnight "and attack the enemy until the last. You have all devoted yourselves to his Majesty the Emperor. Don't think of yourselves. I am at the head of you all." That day Tokyo sent word that Kuribayashi had been promoted to the rank of full general. He did not acknowledge this honor, and he may not have received the message. If he did, he would have known that this was a reward for his gallant stand and that Tokyo was aware that the end had come. That night, General Kuribayashi sent Imperial Headquarters the message it had long dreaded:

> The situation is now on the brink of the end. At midnight of the 17th I shall lead the final offensive, praying that our empire will eventually emerge victorious and secure. I am pleased to report that we have continued to fight well against the overwhelming material power of the enemy, and all my officers and men deserve the highest commendation. I however humbly apologize to His Majesty that I have failed to live up to expectations and have to yield this key island to the enemy after having seen many of my officers and men killed.
>
> Unless this island is wrested back our country won't be secure. Even as a ghost, I wish to be a vanguard of future Japanese operations against this place. Bullets are gone and water exhausted. Now that we are ready for the final act, I am grateful to have been given this opportunity to respond to the gracious will of His Majesty. Permit me to say farewell.
>
> In conclusion, I take the liberty of adding the following clumsy poem:

Shells and bullets are gone and we perish,
Remorseful of failure to fulfill our mission.
My body shall not decay in the field
Unless we are avenged;
I will be born seven more times again
To take up arms against the foe.
My only concern is
Our country in the future
When weeds cover Iwo.

That night a grieving Japanese nation learned that Iwo Jima was lost. Premier Kuniaki Koiso, the leader who had replaced Tojo, told the people: "There will be no unconditional surrender. So long as there is one Japanese living, we must fight to shatter the enemy's ambitions to pieces."

There was no *banzai* charge that night, though. Instead General Kuribayashi with about 400 men came out of hiding—probably from under the blockhouse—and moved to a cave closer to the water. Evidently the general had decided to take a few more Americans with him before going out in a blaze of glory.

Next day the Marines returned to the blockhouse. Tankdozers had now caught up to the riflemen moving through the gorge. Grinding slowly forward while bullets clanged against their steel-plated hides, the tankdozers pushed dirt and rubble over the blockhouse's air vents and sealed them off. The Marine engineers arrived with five enormous charges of dynamite, each weighing 1,600 pounds. Five times Iwo Jima was rocked by great explosions, and with that the blockhouse finally caved in.

The tankdozers and their covering riflemen rolled on. The Gorge was shrinking steadily. It became an area of about 100 square yards, then 80, then 60.... Tankdozers were butting out paths for the Sherman tanks that followed. With their 75-millimeter guns, the Shermans could fire point-blank into the last few cave mouths.

Suddenly, out of one of the caves, came a Japanese soldier. He ran at the tankdozer with a satchel charge. The Marine driver swung his clumsy vehicle around to confront the enemy. Raising his bulldozer blade high in the air, he dropped it, and cut his assailant in two. With that, the driver climbed out of his tankdozer and ran back to the waiting Shermans. Heedless of bullets spanging around him, he hammered on the side of one until the commander opened his turret.

"Did you see what that crazy Nip tried to do to me?" the excited driver yelled. "That does it, brother—I've *had* it!"

He turned and walked out of the gorge.

But he and his comrades were back the following day, March 21, and on that night General Kuribayashi sent a message to the neighboring garrison on the island of Chichi Jima: "We have not eaten nor drunk for five days. But our fighting spirit is still running high. We are going to fight bravely to the last." Three days later, there came another message: "All officers and men of Chichi Jima—good-by."

Those were General Kuribayashi's last words, if indeed they did come from him. No one knows. Nor does anyone know what happened to the Japanese commander. On March 25, the Gorge was down to a square of 50 yards, and on that day a Marine combat patrol traversed it without harm. The end, it seemed, had come.

But in the early-morning darkness of March 26, some 300 shadowy figures clambered from the caves and caverns and holes of the Gorge pocket. Many of them carried sabers, and there were numerous officers among them. Tadamichi Kuribayashi probably was there, perhaps seeing to it that the men who carried explosives knew where they were to go on this final suicide charge. The chief target was the Army Air Corps' VII Fighter Command on the west coast near Airfield Number Two.

There the suiciders came upon troops untrained for fighting on foot. They struck with a howl, throwing grenades, stabbing sleeping airmen, and blasting away with captured American weapons. Then the Japanese overran a battalion of Marine construction troops. There, too, the fighting was confused and bloody, until First Lieutenant Harry Martin rallied the Marines and stopped the enemy short of a hastily organized defense line. Then he broke the Japanese with a countercharge. In the end, Martin was killed. He was the last Marine to win the Medal of Honor on Iwo Jima.

For daylight of March 26 brought the official declaration that Iwo Jima had fallen. Daybreak also revealed 223 Japanese bodies lying in the Airfield Number Two area. The body of Tadamichi Kuribay-ashi was not among them. Nor was it ever found.

So, after 36 days the bitter fighting ended and the weary, grimy, silent victors of Iwo Jima turned to counting the costs. They could be seen in the thousands of crosses and the scores of stars standing in neat white rows in the three divisional cemeteries. They could be counted in the hospital ships which had been sailing daily back to the Marianas and Hawaii.

The 5th Division alone had been staggered by

8,563 casualties. Iwo had been its first and only fight, and few if any outfits have ever been blooded as was the fledgling 5th. And when they buried their dead, among them were three more Medal of Honor winners: Sergeant Joseph Julian, who lost his life charging pillboxes, and Private First Class James LaBelle and Private George Phillips, who threw themselves on grenades to save their comrades.

The sacrifices of these men demonstrated the indomitable spirit of the young American Marines on Iwo Jima. All through the last days of battle the living Marines had been coming down to the cemeteries to acknowledge their debt to the dead. There they knelt or stood with bowed heads in prayerful farewell. Some of them decorated the graves of their buddies. Sometimes they carved crosses out of Iwo's limestone. At other graves they laid Marine emblems or some last salute they had scratched on the bottom of a mess pan with the point of a bayonet. Sometimes inscriptions or designs were made by pressing cartridges into the sand. Some of these epitaphs said:

REACH DOWN, DEAR LORD, FOR THIS MARINE
WHO GAVE HIS ALL THAT WE MIGHT LIVE.

MONTY—A GOOD MARINE WHO DIED IN DEED

'TILL THE LAST MAN

BUT NOT IN VAIN.

And then, as though out of the very heart of the nation, there came this cry of grief:

BUT GOD—FIFTEEN YEARS IS NOT ENOUGH!

In all, 4,189 Marines had been killed in action on Iwo Jima. With another 15,749 men who were wounded or put out of action in one way or another, the total cost had been 19,938 casualties. Yet, as heavy as the American losses were, only a handful of the 21,000 Japanese defenders survived. The death toll favored the attacking Americans by a ratio of more than five to one. This was an astonishing figure, because in war the attacker usually suffers far more than the defender. General Graves Erskine was mindful of this when he paid the last tribute to the fallen.

"Let the world count our crosses!" he said.

"Let them count them over and over. Then when they understand the significance of the fighting for Iwo Jima, let them wonder how *few* there are."

The Marines had not only fought the most ferocious battle in Marine Corps history, but they were the victors of the most savage single struggle in the annals of American arms. But the brave young Marines who sailed away from Iwo Jima shared no feelings of triumph. They felt only a deep sense of sadness and loss. They would never forget the men they had left behind. Nor would the nation ever forget the name of that terrible, bloody place where the flag was flung to the foreign wind and the gateway to Japan torn open.

It was immortal now. It held equal rank with Valley Forge, Gettysburg, Belleau Wood and Guadalcanal.

Fleet Admiral Chester W. Nimitz gave Iwo Jima its epitaph:

"Among the Americans who served on Iwo Jima, uncommon valor was a common virtue."

Order of Events in the Invasion of Iwo Jima

Nov. 24, 1944	B-29s from the Marianas conduct the first land-based aircraft raid on Tokyo
Dec. 8, 1944	Units of the United States Navy shell Iwo Jima. They return to shell the island again on Dec. 27, Jan. 5, and Jan. 24.
Feb. 15-16, 1945	Fifth Amphibious Corps leaves the Marianas after rehearsals for assault on Iwo Jima.
Feb. 16-18, 1945	Supporting naval forces conduct preinvasion bombardment of Iwo Jima with aircraft and gunfire.
Feb. 19, 1945	The 4th and 5th Marine divisions land on Iwo Jima and gain a foothold.

	Seabees land to build roads to battle zone.
Feb. 22, 1945	The 3rd Division's 21st Regiment is committed to battle in the 4th Division's zone.
	Japanese *kamikazes* attack support ships lying off Iwo Jima.
Feb. 23, 1945	The 28th Marines raise the American flag atop Mt. Suribachi.
Feb. 25, 1945	The last units of the 3rd division are committed to the battle.
	The 4th Division enters the "Meatgrinder."
Feb. 27, 1945	The 3rd Division overruns Airfield Number Two and Hill 199.
March 1, 1945	The 5th Division overruns Hill 362A.
	The 3rd Division clears Airfield Number Three

March 3, 1945	Marines of the 5th Division capture Hill 362B.

March 3, 1945   Marines of the 5th Division capture Hill 362B.

March 4, 1945   The Meatgrinder is finally shattered by 4th Division.

The first B-29 lands on Iwo Jima.

March 6, 1945   Air Force P-51 Mustangs and P-61 Black Widows arrive on Iwo.

March 7, 1945   The 3rd Division makes a pre-down attack against Hill 362C, which is captured later that day.

March 8, 1945   Japanese launch *banzai* attack at night and are repulsed with heavy losses.

March 9, 1945   Marines of the 3rd Division reach the other end of Iwo Jima.

March 16, 1945   Last strong enemy opposition is eliminated in 3rd Division's zone with fall of Cushman's Pocket.

	General Kuribayashi informs Toko of the impending loss of Iwo Jima.
March 19, 1945	The 4th Division takes ship for Hawaii.
March 26, 1945	Surviving Japanese launch a desperate early-morning attack against Marine and Army Air Force units near Airfield Number Two.
	The Battle for Iwo Jima is officially declared over.

Note on Unit Strength

Squad	=	10 men
Platoon	=	40 men
Company	=	200 men
Battalion	=	1,000 men
Regiment	=	3,000 men
Division	=	20,000 men
Corps	=	50,000 or more men

In the Marine Corps, four squads make up one platoon; four platoons and a headquarters section make up a company; three companies and a headquarters company make up a battalion; three battalions make up a regiment; and three regiments plus an artillery regiment make up a division.

A Marine division's strength is usually about 20,000 men because, in addition to the "line" (infantry) and artillery regiments, there are many special units attached to the division. These special units include battalions of tanks, engineers, motor transport, and amtracks. In addition there are medical-aid, war-dog, rocket, communication, and intelligence units. Two or more of these big 20,000-man divisions form a corps of upwards of 50,000 men, because a corps also has its specialists of service and supply.

At Iwo jima the Fifth Amphibious Corps included three Marine divisions, the 3rd, 4th, and 5th. In all, this was a force of about 70,000 men.

These figures serve only as approximations, because military units always vary in size. A number of men are always sick, on leave, on loan to other units or going home after being discharged. In one campaign a division may need its tanks; in another, impassable terrain will make it necessary to leave the tanks behind. Thus an army, like the wars it fights, is an inconstant, changing thing.

Marines who Won the Medal of Honor on Iwo Jima

(* indicates that the award was given after death)

Name	Rank	Date	Reason for Award
*Berry, Charles Joseph	Corporal	March 3, 1945	Smothered grenade with his body to save his comrades
*Caddy, William Robert	Private First Class	March 3, 1945	Smothered grenade with his body to save his comrades.
*Cole, Darrell Samuel	Sergeant	Feb. 19, 1945	Fought his way to Airfield One and destroyed several pillboxes before he was killed
Dunlap, Robert Hugo	Captain	Feb. 20-21, 1945	Spent two nights in front of Marine lines, directing fire

			on enemy caves.
Chambers, Justice Marion	Lieutenant	Feb. 19–22, 1945	Exposing himself to Colonel enemy fire he inspired his men in assault on Quarry until he fell critically wounded.
Gray, Ross Franklin	Sergeant	Feb. 21, 1945	Wiped out six enemy positions and killed more than 25 enemy soldiers.
Harrell, William George	Sergeant	March 3, 1945	In dawn battle he saved his post, killing a dozen enemy soldiers, but lost both hands.
Jacobson, Douglas Thomas	Private First Class	Feb. 26, 1945	Destroyed 16 pillboxes and killed 75 Japanese in

			assault on Hill 382.
*Julian, Joseph Rodolph	Sergeant	March 9, 1945	In a one-man assault he smashed enemy positions with grenades, a rifle, demolition charges and a bazooka.
*LaBelle, James Dennis	Private First Class	March 8, 1945	Smothered grenade with his body to save his comrades.
Leims, John Harold	Second Lieutenant	March 7, 1945	Made two trips into enemy area to save wounded men from certain death.
Lucas, Jacklyn Harrell	Private First Class	Feb. 20, 1945	Fell on one grenade, pulled a second under him to save comrades.

*Lummus, Jack	First Lieutenant	March 8, 1945	Destroyed three pillboxes single-handedly. Despite serious wounds he led his men until blown up by land mine.
*Martin, Harry Linn	First Lieutenant	March 26, 1945	Rallied his men and fought off final enemy charge.
McCarthy, Joseph Jeremiah	Captain	Feb. 21, 1945	Knocked out two pillboxes and inspired capture of ridge in front of Airfield Number Two.
*Phillips, George	Private	March 14, 1945	Smothered grenade with his body to save his comrades.
Pierce, Francis Jr.	Corpsman	March 15-16, 1945	Fought off enemy, treated injured even

though
wounded.

*Ruhl, Donald Jack	Private First Class	Feb. 19–21, 1945	After three days of heroic fighting, smothered a demolition charge to save his companion.
Sigler, Franklin Earl	Private	March 14, 1945	Despite wounds he led a fierce assault which destroyed a number of enemy positions; then he directed artillery fire and rescued wounded comrades.
*Stein, Tony	Corporal	Feb. 19, 1945	Killed 20 enemies in slashing d-day assault.
Wahlen, George Edward	Corpsman	Feb. 26, 1945	Wounded three times in saving

			injured Marines.
*Walsh, William Gary	Sergeant	Feb. 27, 1945	Led two daring assaults and then smothered a grenade with his body to save comrades.
Watson, Wilson Douglas	Private	Feb. 26–27, 1945	Destroyed a pillbox and then scaled a ridge and killed 60 Japanese while exposed to enemy fire.
Williams, Hershel Woodrow	Corporal	Feb. 23, 1945	In a four-hour assault smashed several enemy strongpoints with a flame thrower.
*Williams, Jack	Corpsman	March 3, 1945	Shot four times, died still treating Marines.
*Willis, John Harlan	Corpsman	Feb. 28, 1945	Died treating Marine and fighting a grenade battle.